PRAISE F
GETTING IN GOD'S FACE

I'm utterly convinced that God is calling this generation
to pray like never before. To do that, we are going to need
practical resources and the encouragement of people like
Dutch Sheets, who's one of the American godfathers of
intercession. *Getting in God's Face* is an excellent, accessible
introduction to the ancient art of prayer, and I recommend
it as a great starting point for anyone who wants to learn.
I particularly appreciate the way the book builds faith
without resorting to hype and makes complex issues
understandable. There's a lot of excitement out there about
making history and changing the world, but authentic
transformation begins when we stop expecting personalities,
programs and even products to save the planet, and look
solely to Jesus in prayer. I guarantee that this book really
won't change the world. But if you buy it, read it and do
what it says—someone like you really could.

PETE GREIG
LEADER, 24-7 PRAYER
AUTHOR, *RED MOON RISING*

This book needs to get into the hands of every student on every
campus if we are going to see another youth revival in our
nation. I have been contending for revival on campuses for years
and never have I seen students hunger to experience God in
prayer more than right now. All across the nation there has been
a growing hunger among students to not only pray but to
understand how to pray. *Getting in God's Face* by Dutch Sheets is
timely and needed. Students can't just hunger for prayer, they
need to know how to pray effectively; and this book is the
answer! Intercession will be the key to release heaven on Earth
in this generation. May this book fan the fire of revival prayer
into the heart of every student who reads it. May it be used to
spark a new great awakening to save the youth of our nation!

JAESON MA
LEAD DIRECTOR, CAMPUS CHURCH NETWORKS

GETTING IN
GOD'S FACE

Dutch Sheets

Regal

From Gospel Light
Ventura, California, U.S.A.

PUBLISHED BY REGAL BOOKS
FROM GOSPEL LIGHT
VENTURA, CALIFORNIA, U.S.A.
PRINTED IN THE U.S.A.

Regal Books is a ministry of Gospel Light, a Christian publisher dedicated to serving the local church. We believe God's vision for Gospel Light is to provide church leaders with biblical, user-friendly materials that will help them evangelize, disciple and minister to children, youth and families.

It is our prayer that this Regal book will help you discover biblical truth for your own life and help you meet the needs of others. May God richly bless you.

For a free catalog of resources from Regal Books/Gospel Light, please call your Christian supplier or contact us at 1-800-4-GOSPEL or www.regalbooks.com.

Library of Congress Cataloging-in-Publication Data
Sheets, Dutch.
  Getting in God's face / Dutch Sheets.
    p. cm.
  ISBN 0-8307-3801-0 (trade paper)
  1. Prayer—Christianity. I. Title.

BV210.3.S545 2006
248.3'2—dc22   2006013345

Rights for publishing this book in other languages are contracted by Gospel Light Worldwide, the international nonprofit ministry of Gospel Light. Gospel Light Worldwide also provides publishing and technical assistance to international publishers dedicated to producing Sunday School and Vacation Bible School curricula and books in the languages of the world. For additional information, visit www.gospellightworldwide.org; write to Gospel Light Worldwide, P.O. Box 3875, Ventura, CA 93006; or send an e-mail to info@gospellightworldwide.org.

CONTENTS

CHAPTER 1 7
Ask Away

CHAPTER 2 13
God Doesn't *Really* Need Our Prayers, Does He?

CHAPTER 3 27
Representin' Jesus

CHAPTER 4 41
Meetings: The Good, the Bad and the Ugly

CHAPTER 5 53
I Get By with a Little Help from My Friends

CHAPTER 6 63
No Trespassing

CHAPTER 7 73
Butterflies, Mice, Elephants and Bull's-Eyes

CHAPTER 8 85
Supernatural Childbirth

CHAPTER 9 97
How to Become a Pro Wrestler

CHAPTER 10 109
War Tactics

CHAPTER 11 123
The Lightning of God

CHAPTER 12 135
The Substance of Prayer

CHAPTER 13 147
A Vision of You

DISCUSSION LEADER'S GUIDE 153

ASK AWAY

CHAPTER 1

I knew that the girl I was going to pray for was really sick. What I didn't know was that she was comatose, with a tracheostomy in her throat and a feeding tube in her stomach. She'd been in that condition for a year and a half. Seeing her for the first time was like expecting a prescription and receiving brain surgery. Her sister, who had asked me to visit this young lady, hadn't given me the whole story for fear I wouldn't go at all. She knew if she could just get me there once, I'd probably go back. She was right!

The doctors gave Angie no hope for living, let alone coming out of the coma. Even if she did regain consciousness, doctors said she'd basically be a "vegetable" because of her extensive brain damage.

I don't know if you've ever stood beside someone in this kind of condition and asked God for a miracle, but it can be pretty intimidating. It can also teach you a lot—about life and death, about yourself and about our God, especially when you stand beside the same person 60 to 70 times, for an hour or more each time, throughout the course of a year.

Um, This Isn't How I Planned It

Things didn't work out as I had expected. I figured the Lord would heal this young lady through our prayers in a dramatic, easy, quick way. After all, that's how it happened with Jesus, wasn't it? He'd say the words with just the right amount of faith—and voilá!

What ended up happening was that I prayed with a completely unresponsive person for three or four hours of my life each week for a year. I experienced humiliation and insults from the staff of the nursing home where she stayed. Tears . . . frustrating moments . . . times of boldness . . . times of intimidation. I never imagined the process taking so long or teaching me so much.

But one day it finally happened. The front page of the local paper read "Woman Awake, Alive, Healthy After Two Years in Coma." Doctors called it a "medical miracle." "We have no explanation," they said, though they stopped short of giving God the glory.

Yes, God restored Angie. He healed her brain—the outer layer of which those same doctors said had been totally destroyed by a virus. Every part of it had been covered with infection.

It actually happened on a Saturday morning when Angie was alone. Earlier that week she had been moved from the nursing home to a hospital for treatment of an infection. After administering more tests, the doctors determined that her condition had grown worse and informed her family that she'd probably die soon.

As soon as Angie's sister told me this, I dashed off to the hospital to speak to Angie. "This nightmare is almost over," I said, with tears streaming down my face. "Nothing can keep us from receiving our miracle. Nothing!"

The memory is forever imprinted on my mind. As I exited the hospital weeping, I remember saying to myself again and again, "Nothing can keep us from our miracle. Nothing!"

It wasn't just a strong kind of hope I had at this point; it was great faith. I had turned to God many times throughout the

NO ONE IS BORN A PRAYER HERO

In *The Last Days Newsletter,* Leonard Ravenhill told about a group of tourists visiting a picturesque village who walked by an old man sitting beside a fence. In a rather patronizing way, one tourist asked, "Were any great men born in this village?"

The old man replied, "Nope, only babies."[1]

course of that year asking Him if He'd really sent me to this girl. Each time I received His assurance: "I sent you. Don't quit."

PERSISTENTLY ASKING

A lack of endurance is one of the greatest causes of defeat, especially when it comes to prayer. We don't wait well. While we're into microwaving, God, on the other hand, is usually into marinating. So I persisted for a year, and my faith grew until I knew deep inside that we were going to win. My motto had become Galatians 6:9: "Let us not lose heart in doing good, for in due time we shall reap if we do not grow weary."

My persistence was rewarded when, three days after that Wednesday in the hospital, Angie woke up with her brain *completely* healed. It was a genuine miracle—one that had people around the world calling the nursing home and asking about her incredible recovery.

But that and other prayer journeys that I've since been on have stirred up what seems to be a billion questions inside me—all about prayer. They're questions everyone has, such as:

- Is prayer really necessary? If so, why? Isn't God sovereign? Doesn't that mean He can do what He wants, when He wants? Then why should I pray?
- Why does it often take so long to get a prayer answered? Why is persistence required? Am I supposed to wrestle with God like Jacob did, or do I just stick to the easy prayers?
- What about praying for my non-Christian friends? I thought God *wanted* to save them. Then why do I feel as though I'm trying to talk Him into it?
- What about spiritual warfare? If Satan is defeated and Christ has all authority, shouldn't I just forget about the

devil? Does God bind the devil, or do I?

- What exactly is intercessory prayer? And don't just tell me it's "standing in the gap." Enough spiritual jargon— what does "intercessory" mean?
- What about protection? Is everything that happens to me or my family simply allowed by God? Or is there something I need to do to make sure we're safe?
- What's all this talk about "bearing one another's burdens" (Gal. 6:2)?
- Is there a right time for answers to prayer, or does the timing depend on me?

FOR EVERY GOOD QUESTION THERE'S A GOOD ANSWER

Tired of all these questions? Tired of not getting any answers? A lot of people get so sick of the tough questions that they stop asking them—and stop praying, too.

Please don't do that!

Keep asking! I've discovered that the right answer begins with the right question. I've also discovered that God is not offended by a sincere question. He loves an honest seeker. And He's big enough to answer the toughies. He really is a good Dad.

So before we go any farther on our journey to find our Father's answers to some of these big questions about prayer, let's ask Him for help.

PRAYER IN PRACTICE

Father, thank You for being approachable and for letting me come to You with hard questions. I admit that I don't need any more head knowledge—I need understanding. I need Your truth, because sometimes the Bible seems to contradict my daily

*experiences, especially when it comes to prayer. Sometimes it's
hard to believe that You are actually listening when I've prayed
the same prayer again and again and again.*

*So just like Your disciples did, Lord, I'm asking that You teach
me to pray. I'm tired of the pretending and all the spiritual
games; I want the real thing. I'm sick of praying prayers that
just sound or feel good but have no results. I want to pray
what's on Your heart, with Your power.*

Help me on this journey, Lord. In Jesus' name, I pray.

Amen.

THINGS THAT MAKE YA GO HMM . . .

1. Have you ever prayed for something but didn't get any results? What did you pray for? Why do you think your prayer wasn't answered?
2. Explain your take on what prayer is.
3. Who is the most effective pray-er you've ever seen? Why do you think his or her prayers are answered?

Note

1. Craig Brian Larson, *Illustrations for Preaching and Teaching* (Grand Rapids, MI: Baker Books, 1993), p. 128.

GOD DOESN'T *REALLY* NEED OUR PRAYERS, DOES HE?

CHAPTER 2

$\mathbf{B}$ecause I said so!"

Don't you just hate it when people (especially your parents) say this as the reason for doing something? Not only is it frustrating to hear, but it's also the ultimate motivation killer—especially when you sincerely want to know why. I remember as a kid getting my knuckles rapped with a ruler for asking the simple question "Why?"

Whack! "Because I said so! Now be quiet and do it."

I still wish I could rap that teacher's knuckles with a yardstick and not tell *her* why! (OK, so maybe that's not the most Christian thing for a pastor to say. Don't worry, we'll deal with forgiveness and inner healing another time.)

The truth is, none of us wants to do something just because someone else said so. And it's no different when it comes to a major part of following God: prayer.

IT'S OK TO ASK WHY

Understanding the why of doing something can be a great motivating force. But the opposite is also true. As a kid, I wondered why the sign said "No Diving" in the shallow end of the pool. Then one day I dove in and hit my head on the bottom. I don't do that anymore.

I used to wonder why I shouldn't touch the pretty red glow on the stove. I found out.

I wondered why a guy in front of me in the woods said, "Duck." I thought, *I don't want to duck. I don't have to duck.* Then the branch whopped me upside the head. Now I duck.

Thankfully, God understands our inquisitive nature. That's why He gave us a user's guide full of answers to the *whys* of life. It's called the Bible and, despite what others around you might believe, it's *completely* relevant to your life. God doesn't expect us to live like robots, always doing what we're told without ever asking why.

IS PRAYER REALLY NECESSARY?

If God is going to do something regardless of whether or not we pray, then He doesn't need us to ask, and we don't need to waste our time. Right? We've got enough to do. If it's all *que sera, sera* (whatever will be, will be), then why not take a siesta and just let it all happen?

If, on the other hand, John Wesley was correct when he said, "God does nothing on the earth save in answer to believing prayer," then I'll lose a little sleep for that. I'll change my lifestyle for that. I'll turn the TV off, set my cell phone on mute, ignore the IMs, and even miss a meal or two.

So the real question is this: Does a sovereign, all-powerful God need our involvement or not? Is prayer really necessary? If so, why?

IS GOD PLAYING GAMES?

Why do we have to pray? I'm not talking about just asking for stuff. Obviously we ask because we want or need something. But think about it: If God sees everything and already knows what's best for me, why should I bother asking for anything? Do my prayers really matter all that much? Isn't God going to do what He wants anyway?

Can my prayers actually change things? Does God *need* me to pray or does He just *want* me to pray? Some people would argue that an all-powerful God doesn't "need" anything, including our prayers. So what gives? (Keep reading for the answers.)

I believe that prayer is necessary. Our prayers *can* bring change. They *can* bring healing, reconciliation, transformation, miracles—the possibilities are as endless as God Himself. How do I know this? Read on.

GOD'S PLAN A

The answer to why prayer is necessary lies in God's original plan when He created Adam. The word "Adam" means "man; human being."[1] In other words, God made man and called him "Man." He made a human and called him "Human." He made an adam and named him "Adam." In fact, often when the Bible uses the term "man," the actual Hebrew word is *adam,* spelled just like our English word. I share this simply to say that Adam represents all of us. What God intended for Adam, He intended for the entire human race.

What was God's intention? Initially, He gave Adam and Eve and their descendants dominion over the entire earth and over all creation, as we see in Genesis 1:26-28:

> Then God said, "Let Us make man in Our image, according to Our likeness; and let them rule over the fish of the sea and over the birds of the sky and over the cattle and over all the earth, and over every creeping thing that creeps on the earth." And God created man in His own image, in the image of God He created him; male and female He created them. And God blessed them; and God said to them, "Be fruitful and multiply, and fill the earth, and subdue it; and rule over the fish of the sea and over the birds of the sky, and over every living thing that moves on the earth."

We see this also in Psalm 8:3-8:

When I consider Your heavens, the work of Your fingers, the moon and the stars, which You have ordained; What is man that You take thought of him, and the son of man that You care for him? Yet You have made him a little lower than God, and You crown him with glory and majesty! You make him to rule over the works of Your hands; You have put all things under his feet, all sheep and oxen, and also the beasts of the field, the birds of the heavens and the fish of the sea, whatever passes through the paths of the seas.

RE-PRESENTIN' GOD

In Psalm 8:6, the original Hebrew word used for "rule" is *mashal*. It indicates that Adam was God's *manager* here, God's *steward* or *governor*. Adam was God's *mediator, go-between* or *representative*.

Psalm 115:16 confirms this: "The heaven . . . the Eternal holds himself, the earth He has *assigned* to men" (*Moffatt*, emphasis added). God didn't give away ownership of the earth, but He did assign the responsibility of governing it to humanity. Think of it like the manager of a baseball team who's assigned to lead, organize and coach a group of players. That manager ultimately represents the owner of the team; in a way, you could say he's the "face" of the owner.

But what does it actually mean to represent someone? The dictionary defines representation as "to present again."[2] Another way to say it might be to *re*-present someone. A representative is one who re-presents the will of another. For instance, a baseball manager re-presents the will of his owner to his players. While he's in charge of planning the Xs and Os for the team, he coaches according to the will of his owner.

The dictionary gives a few other meanings for "represent": "to exhibit the image and counterpart of; to speak and act with authority on the part of; to be a substitute or agent for."[3] Sounds similar to what God told Adam, doesn't it?

Now, it's no small task to re-present God. So to help humans carry out this assignment, God made us so much like Himself that it was scary. "And God created man in His own image, in the image of God He created him; male and female He created them" (Gen. 1:27). The Hebrew word for "image" is *tselem*, which involves the concept of a "shadow," a "phantom" or an "illusion."[4]

An illusion is something you think you see, but on closer observation you discover that your eyes have tricked you. When the rest of creation saw Adam, they must've done a double take: *Man, I could've sworn I saw God—oh, it's just Adam.* How's that for re-presentation?

We're also told that Adam was *similar to* or *comparable to* God. The Hebrew word *demuwth*, translated "likeness" in Genesis 1:26, comes from the root word *damah*, meaning "to compare."[5] Adam was very much like God!

Psalm 8:5 actually says human beings were made just "a little lower than God" and that we were crowned with God's very own glory. The definition of the Hebrew word *kabowd* that's translated "glory" literally means "heavy or weighty"![6] It's linked to the concept of authority. We still use the picture today when we refer to someone who "carries a lot of weight." Adam carried God's weight on the earth. I don't know what Adam weighed but he was heavy. He represented God with full authority! He was large and in charge!

The Greek word for glory, *doxa*, is just as loaded. It involves the concept of recognition. More specifically, it's what causes someone (or something) to be recognized for who he or she (or it) really is.[7] When we read in Scripture that humankind is the glory of God (see 1 Cor. 11:7), it's telling us that God was *recognized* in humans. Why? So humans could accurately *represent* Him. When creation looked at Adam, they were supposed to see God.

And they did! That is, until Adam sinned and couldn't carry the weight of God's glory anymore. God is no longer recognized in fallen humankind. We have to be changed back into God's image "from glory to glory" (2 Cor. 3:18) for others to recognize God in us again.

HELP! I'M DROWNING IN VERBIAGE!

OK, enough definitions. You'll find through the rest of this book that I like to examine words and their original meanings to reveal a deeper meaning that's often overlooked. My point isn't to overwhelm you with a bunch of new words in another language. By looking deeper into how the Bible was originally written, we can broaden our understanding of God's plan for humankind at the Creation. Let's recap based on what we've learned so far:

Adam was comparable to or similar to God—so much like God that it was illusionary. God was recognized in Adam, which meant that Adam "carried the weight" here on Earth. Adam represented God, presenting again His will on the earth. Adam was God's governor or manager here. The earth was Adam's assignment; it was under Adam's charge or care. How things went on planet Earth, for better or worse, depended on Adam and his offspring.

Think about that. If the earth remained a paradise, it would be because of humankind. If things became messed up, it would be because of humankind. If the serpent ever gained control, it would be because of humankind. Humanity really was in charge!

Why would God do it this way? Why would He take such a risk? From what I know about God in the Scriptures and from my personal walk with Him, it comes down to one thing: God wanted a family—sons and daughters who could personally relate to Him, and vice versa. So He made our original parents similar to Himself. He put His very life and Spirit into them, gave them a sweet crib by the beach with lots of exotic pets, sat down and said, "This is good." Every day He would hang out with them, walk with them, teach them about Himself and their home. He said, "Give me some grandsons and granddaughters." God was now a dad, and He was thrilled!

A HEFTY PRICE FOR A BAD MISTAKE

What's the point of all this? Check this out: God assigned so much authority over the earth to Adam that he, not just God, had the ability to give it away! In fact, when Adam did exactly that—giving it away to Satan and making him "the ruler of this world" (see John 12:31; 14:30; 16:11)—it cost God big time. Jesus had to become a part of the human race to fix the mess Adam made. The Father had to give up His only Son. If that doesn't prove God's love and determination to use us through thick or thin, then I don't know what does. Without question, *God made us to always be His link to authority and activity on the earth.*

And that's why prayer is necessary. God chose, from the time of the Creation, to work on the earth *through* humans, not independent of them. He always has and always will, even at the cost of becoming one. Though God is sovereign and all-powerful, Scripture clearly tells us that He limited Himself in order to work through human beings. That's one of the major points of the entire Bible.

Does God really *need* us? Yes and no. Because He's God, He's already complete (see Acts 17:24-25). He doesn't lack a thing (see Job 41:11; Ps. 50:10-12). But because of His desire to be in an authentic relationship with us, He's chosen to limit Himself by working through us. In essence, He set up a situation where He actually *needs* us.

Still, a few questions remain. Does He really need us to ask for His kingdom to come, His will to be done (see Matt. 6:10)? Surely He wouldn't want us to waste our time asking for something that was going to happen anyway, would He?

Didn't He tell us to ask for our daily bread (see Matt. 6:11)? And yet He knows what we need before we even ask.

Didn't He tell us to ask for people to help save the lost (see Matt. 9:38)? But doesn't the Lord want to see people saved even more than we do?

Basically, all these things point to a single question: Why am I supposed to ask God for something He already wants to do? Could it be that my asking somehow releases Him to do it? Believe it or not, that's not so out there. In fact, there are at least three significant passages in the Bible that support this.

A PRAYING PROPHET

In 1 Kings 18, we find the story of God needing and using a person to accomplish His will through prayer. After three years of severe drought, God spoke to the prophet Elijah and said, "Go, show yourself to Ahab, and I will send rain on the face of the earth" (v. 1). By the end of this chapter, after several other events have occurred, Elijah prays seven times and the rain finally comes.

But think about it: Whose idea was it to send rain? Whose will? Whose initiation? (I'll give you a hint: It wasn't Elijah's.)

So if it was God's will, idea and timing, why did it take a human's prayers to bring rain? Did Elijah's prayers really produce the rain or was it simply coincidental that he happened to be praying when God sent it?

James answers this last question with a resounding YES! The "effectual fervent prayer" of the prophet stopped and brought the rain:

Elijah was a man with a nature like ours, and he prayed earnestly that it might not rain; and it did not rain on the earth for three years and six months. And he prayed again, and the sky poured rain, and the earth produced its fruit (Jas. 5:17-18).

The only logical answer to the question of why Elijah needed to pray is simply that *God has chosen to work through people.* Even when the Lord Himself initiates something, He still needs us to ask.

NOT JUST LION'S FOOD

Another example that indicates the absolute need for prayer is found in the life of Daniel. In 606 B.C., Israel had been taken captive by another nation because of its sin. Years later, as recorded in the book of Daniel, chapter 9, we're told that while reading the prophet Jeremiah, Daniel discovered it was time for Israel's captivity to end. Not only had Jeremiah prophesied the captivity of which Daniel was a part, but he had also prophesied the exact duration: 70 years.

At this point Daniel got radical on us. When we receive an incredible promise from God, most of us tend to just passively wait for it to come about. But not Daniel. He knew better. Somehow he must have known that God needed his involvement, because he said, "So I gave my attention to the Lord God

"God's giving is inseparably connected with our asking. . . . Only by intercession can that power be brought down from heaven, which will enable the Church to conquer the world." —Andrew Murray[8]

to seek Him by prayer and supplications, with fasting, sackcloth, and ashes" (Dan. 9:3).

Unlike with Elijah, there's nothing that specifically says Israel was restored because of Daniel's prayers. But with the emphasis given to them, it's certainly implied. We do know that the angel Gabriel was dispatched immediately after Daniel started praying. However, it took him 21 days to penetrate the warfare in the heavens with the message to inform Daniel that "your words were heard, and I have come in response to your words" (Dan. 10:12). I can't help wondering how many promises from God go unfulfilled because He can't find the human involvement He needs.

ON THE LOOKOUT

We find the third example of God's needing a person's prayers in the book of Ezekiel.

> "And I searched for a man among them who should build up the wall and stand in the gap before Me for the land, that I should not destroy it; but I found no one. Thus I have poured out My indignation on them; I have consumed them with the fire of My wrath; their way I have brought upon their heads," declares the Lord God (Ezek. 22:30-31).

This may not seem like a case where God is declaring His need for our prayers, but let's dig deeper. We'll see that what these verses are really saying is staggering.

God's holiness, integrity and uncompromising truth prevent Him from simply excusing sin. It must be judged. On the other hand, not only is He holy, but He is also loving, and His love always desires to redeem, restore and show mercy. Scripture tells us that

God takes no pleasure in the death of the wicked (see Ezek. 33:11).

In essence, God is saying in this passage, "While My justice demanded judgment, My love wanted forgiveness. If I could've found a human to ask Me to spare this people, I would have. It would've allowed Me to show mercy. But because I found no one, I had to destroy them."

Ouch! I don't like the implications of this passage any more than you do. I don't want the responsibility of being "the last hope" for God. And I don't like to consider the ramifications of a God who has somehow limited Himself to us Earthlings. But in light of these and other passages, as well as the condition of the world, it's hard to come to any other conclusion.

Either God wants the earth in this condition or He doesn't. If He doesn't, which is certainly the case, then we have to assume one of two things. Either He is powerless to do anything about it, or He needs and is waiting on something from us to bring about change. In fact, our heavenly Father has placed us in a position of partnership in doing His kingdom work. What an incredible opportunity we have! The Creator of the universe, simply because of His love for us, wants us to work *alongside* Him. He doesn't want us just following a list of dos and don'ts—he wants a real friendship that's based on love.

You and I have the chance of a lifetime. We can rise to the occasion and embrace the incredible invitation to be co-laborers with God, to be carriers of His awesome Holy Spirit and ambassadors for His great kingdom. It's time to start representin'!

PRAYER IN PRACTICE

Lord God, I'm blown away by Your decision to use humans.
As messed up as we are, You still love us enough to limit
Yourself and work through us. Thank You, thank You. Life seems
full of purpose, knowing that there's a reason for praying—

that I'm not just saying lines to a script that's already been plotted out. Help me to take to heart Your need for people You can use. Lead me through the rest of this book to discover how to truly partner with You and pray the things on Your heart. Amen.

THINGS THAT MAKE YA GO HMM...

1. How much authority did God give Adam on the earth? What happened to that power?
2. What did God mean when He said we were made in His image and likeness?
3. How does the story of Elijah's praying for rain show that God works through prayer? How about Daniel's prayer for the restoration of Israel?
4. In your own words, explain why God would limit Himself to use us as part of His plan.
5. How can you be a partner with God?

Notes

1. James Strong, *The New Strong's Exhaustive Concordance of the Bible* (Nashville, TN: Thomas Nelson Publishers, 1990), ref. no. 120.
2. *The Consolidated Webster Encyclopedic Dictionary* (Chicago, IL: Consolidated Book Publishers, 1954), p. 615.
3. Ibid.
4. Spiros Zodhiates, *Hebrew-Greek Key Study Bible—New American Standard* (Chattanooga, TN: AMG Publishers, 1984; revised edition, 1990), p. 1768.
5. Strong, *The New Strong's Exhaustive Concordance*, ref. no. 1819.
6. R. Laird Harris, Gleason L. Archer Jr., and Bruce K. Waltke, *Theological Wordbook of the Old Testament* (Chicago, IL: Moody Press, 1980; Grand Rapids, MI: William B. Eerdmans Publishing Co., revised edition, 1991), p. 426.
7. Zodhiates, *Hebrew-Greek Key Study Bible*, p. 1826.
8. Andrew Murray, *The Ministry of Intercessory Prayer* (Minneapolis, MN: Bethany House Publishers, 1981), pp. 22-23.

REPRESENTIN'
JESUS

CHAPTER 3

So you picked up this book thinking that it might help you learn how to pray. Or maybe you just want to know how to pray better. Maybe you're sick of your prayers never making a difference, and the book's cover content sounded pretty sweet. I mean, who wouldn't want to influence how God works on Earth?

But before we get into tossing mountains and oceans around like Yoda with the Force, we need to clarify a few things. What is intercession anyway?

Nope, you're wrong.

Sorry—didn't mean to cut you off, but if you're like 99.9 percent of the people who answer that question, you said that intercession is prayer or something similar. Technically speaking, intercession isn't prayer at all.

What?! That's downright blasphemous, isn't it? Next thing you know, I'll be telling you to send me all your money for a prayer cloth. Seriously, there's a major difference between intercession and prayer.

NOT ANOTHER DEFINITION! (TRUST ME, THIS ONE'S REALLY IMPORTANT)

in-ter-cede \ vi : *to go or pass between; to act between parties with a view to reconcile those who differ or contend; to interpose; to mediate or make intercession; mediation*[1]

med-i-ate \vb : *between two extremes; to interpose between parties as the equal friend of each; to negotiate between persons at variance with a view to reconciliation; to mediate a peace; intercession*[2]

Notice anything similar with these two definitions? Both use some of the same words—"between," "interpose" and "reconcile." But did you see how one word is used to define the other? Mediation defines intercession and intercession defines mediation.

Intercession happens in our courts daily with lawyers interceding for clients.

It happens in contractual meetings, with attorneys representing one party to another.

It happens in offices and business meetings as secretaries or other associates "go between," representing one to another. Nothing spiritual about it.

Intercession involves delegation.

It involves authority.

It boils down to representation. As we discussed in the previous chapter, to represent means to re-present, or to present again.

Many years ago, my dad hired an intercessor (we called him a lawyer) to represent him in court. Dad had been stopped by some policemen, beaten up pretty badly and thrown in jail—all of this with my mother and then three-year-old sister watching. The policemen thought he was someone else! Dad was actually on his way home from a church service where he had preached that night, which added to the irony and injustice of the entire ordeal.

Our attorney went *between* Dad, the judge, the other lawyer and the policemen. He listened to the case, gathered proof, found out what Dad wanted and then *re-presented* it in court. And he *mediated* well.

We won.

Intercession isn't limited to a legal court case. That's only one example. Any work of representation or mediation between is intercession.

DRAWING A PICTURE OF GOD

Now, let's think about intercession in light of the Creation and the Fall. We learned in the last chapter that Adam was supposed to represent God on planet Earth—managing, governing or ruling for Him. God told Adam what He wanted, and Adam re-presented Him to the rest of the earth. Adam was a go-between for God. Literally, Adam was God's intercessor or mediator on Earth.

Adam, of course, screwed up, and God had to send another human, called the "last Adam," to do what the first Adam was supposed to do. So Christ came to re-present God on Earth. He became the intercessor or mediator, going between and re-presenting God to humanity all over again.

According to John 1:18, Jesus explained God to us: "No man has seen God at any time; the only begotten God, who is in the bosom of the Father, He has explained Him."

It's like the little boy who "was drawing a picture and his teacher said, 'That's an interesting picture. Tell me about it.'

'It's a picture of God.'

'But nobody knows what God looks like.'

'They will when I get done,'" said the young artist.[3]

Jesus came and drew us a picture of God! Now we know what He looks like.

ROOTING FOR BOTH TEAMS

But there's more to the story involving intercession. Check this out: Jesus—the last Adam—came to be God's intercessor, mediator or representative on Earth. But in order to be saved, man needed someone to mediate for him before God. So not only did Christ represent God to man, but He also represented man to God. This God-Man was the attorney for both sides!

Jesus is the ultimate, final and only go-between. He is "the Apostle [God to the human race] and High Priest [the human race to God] of our confession" (Heb. 3:1). He hangs between heaven and Earth, placing one hand on God and the other on humans (see Job 9:32-33).

The New Testament refers to Jesus as always interceding in heaven before the Father on our behalf. People make this out to be as if Jesus were fervently praying away, night and day, for each of us. But His intercession isn't a *prayer* He prays; it's His *work* of mediation (see 1 Tim. 2:5). He's simply being our Advocate with the Father. He is now functioning as our representative, guaranteeing our access to the Father and to our benefits of redemption.

In fact, Jesus tells us in John 16:26 that He isn't doing our asking or petitioning of the Father for us: "In that day you will ask in My name, and I do not say to you that I will request the Father on your behalf." So if He's not begging the Father on our behalf, then what's He doing as He makes intercession for us? He is mediating, or going between, not to clear us of charges against us as He did to redeem us from sin, but to present each of us to the Father as righteous and one of His own.

When I approach the Father's throne, Jesus is always there saying something such as: "Father, Dutch is here to speak with You. He isn't coming on his own merits or righteousness; he's here based on Mine. He is here *in My name*. I'm sure You remember that I've *gone between* You and Dutch and provided him with access to You. He has a few things to ask You."

Can't you just hear the Father say in response, "Of course, I remember, Son. You've made him one of Ours. Because he came through You, Dutch is always welcome here." He then looks at me and says, "Come boldly to My throne of grace, son, and make your request known."

"My little children, I am writing these things to you so that you may not sin. And if anyone sins, we have an Advocate with the Father, Jesus Christ the righteous." —1 John 2:1

Jesus isn't *praying* for us; He is *interceding* for us so that we can pray. This is what is meant by asking "in His name."

THE ONE AND ONLY

There's one more amazing thing that Jesus' intercession does for us. Not only does it *reconcile* us with the Father, but it also *separates* us from the grip of Satan. Jesus is the only one with the authority to present us to the Father, and He's the only one with the rightful power to tell the enemy, "Hands off!" when it comes to messing with our soul's destination. Because of His redemptive work on the cross, Christ is the *one and only* intercessor. This is why the Scriptures say, "For there is one God, and one mediator also between God and men, the man Christ Jesus" (1 Tim. 2:5). This verse could just as easily read "one intercessor."

This revelation is critical. It means that our *prayers* of intercession are always and only an extension of His *work* of intercession. Why is this so important? Because God won't honor any intercession except Christ's (remember, He's the only one who is righteous enough), and also because this understanding will make our *prayers* of intercession infinitely more powerful.

Let's go back to our conversation in the throne room. Imagine I'm there asking the Father to extend mercy and bring salvation to the people of Tibet. The Father could reply, "How can I do this? They're sinners. They worship false gods, which is really worshiping Satan. And besides, they don't even want Me to do this. They've never asked me for themselves."

I answer, "Because Jesus *interceded* or *mediated* for them, Father. I'm asking based on what He did. And He needs a human on Earth to ask for Him because He's in heaven now. So, as He taught me, I'm asking for Your kingdom to come and Your will to be done in Tibet. I'm asking for some laborers to be sent there.

I'm asking these things for Christ and through Christ. And I am asking You to do it based entirely on the redemptive work He has already done."

The Father replies, "RIGHT ANSWER! You heard the man, Gabriel. What are you waiting for?"

GOD, INC.

Is this making a little more sense now? Think of it as if we were traveling the country in a GOD company truck, giving out fresh packets of GOD to eager customers. We're not on the production side. We don't have to *make* anything. We simply distribute what God has already done, as the disciples did with the loaves and fishes (see Matt. 14:17-19).

We don't deliver anyone from spiritual strongholds. We don't reconcile anyone to God. We don't defeat the enemy. The work is already done. Reconciliation is complete. Deliverance and victory are complete. Salvation is complete. Intercession is complete! Finished . . . done . . . WOW! What a relief.

But here's the catch: We have to *ask* for the release and application of these things. And that's what intercessory prayer is. It's us, as the Body (the Church), being an extension of Jesus' work to mediate between God and people in order to save them. At the same time, we serve as Jesus-in-the-flesh when it comes to standing in the gap between Satan and his attempt to destroy as many people as possible. And how do we do that? By simply declaring the victory Jesus has already won by His death and resurrection.

Our calling and function isn't to replace God, but to release Him.[4]

SENT OUT

Christ needs a human on the earth through which to represent Himself, just as the Father did. The Father's human was Jesus; Jesus' humans are us, the Church. He said, "As the Father has sent Me, I also send you" (John 20:21).

As believers, we've all been sent. Unfortunately, few of us really know what our assignment is. Think about it. People who are sent have authority as long as they represent the sender. When your mom instructs you to tell your little sister that her time's up on the computer, you're not just speaking your own words; you're relaying a message that has additional weight because it's straight from Mom. The importance or emphasis isn't on you, the sent one, but on your mother, the sender.

Jesus was a sent one. That's why He had extra *umph* behind everything He said and did. His authority came straight from the Father who sent Him. Forty times in John's Gospel alone, Jesus mentions the important fact of being sent by the Father. The result of this arrangement was that, essentially, He wasn't doing the works—the Father who sent Him was (see John 14:10).

The same is true with us. Our authority comes from being sent ones, representing Jesus. As long as we function in that capacity, we function in Christ's authority. And, in essence, we're not really doing the works—He is.

Let me illustrate. Several years ago, while praying about an upcoming journey to Guatemala, I heard the words: *On this trip, represent Jesus to the people.*

At first I didn't take notice. But the voice came again, this time adding the words: *Be His voice, be His hands, be His feet. Do what you know He would do if He were there in the flesh. Represent Him.*

Suddenly I understood. I wasn't going to represent myself or the ministry with which I was working. In the same way that Jesus represented the Father, speaking His words and doing His works, I was to represent Jesus. And if I really believed I was functioning as an ambassador or a sent one, then I could believe it wasn't my authority or ability that was an issue, but Christ's. I was simply representing Him *and what He had already done.*

A PRAYER FOR THE INSANE

When I got to Guatemala, I traveled with a team to a remote village far from any modern city. There was no electrical power, no plumbing, no phones. We were there to build shelters for the villagers whose homes had been destroyed in a recent earthquake that had killed 30,000 people and left almost a million homeless. We had trucked in materials and were building small one-room homes for them during the daylight hours. In the evenings we would hold services in the center of the village, preaching the gospel of Jesus Christ to them, explaining that His love was motivating us to spend our time, money and energies helping them.

We had been ministering for one week, with very few people coming to Christ. The people were listening but not responding.

I was supposed to preach on the final night of our trip. Just as the service was about to begin, a team member told me about something he and others had found on the far side of the village—a little girl, six or seven years old, tied to a tree.

Not believing what they were seeing, they asked the family that lived there, "Why is this small girl tied to that tree?" It was obvious that she lived there, much like a dog, in the backyard—nasty, filthy, helpless and alone.

"She's crazy," the parents replied. "We can't control her. She hurts herself and others and runs away if we turn her loose. There's nothing else we can do for her, so we just have to tie her up."

My heart broke as the team member shared what he had seen. It was on my mind as we began the service. A few minutes into my message, standing on a folding table under the stars, the same voice that had spoken to me before the trip began speaking to me again.

Tell them that you are going to pray for the little girl across the village tied to the tree. Tell them that you are going to do it in the name of this Jesus you've been preaching about. Tell them that through Him you are going to break the evil powers controlling her—that when she is free and normal, they can then know that what you are preaching is true. They can believe that the Jesus you are preaching about is who you say He is.

I responded to the voice in my heart with fear and trembling. I believe the words were something like, SAY *WHAT?*

Same instructions.

Being the man of faith that I am, I replied, *So what's Plan B?*

I heard, *Remember what I said to you before the trip began? Represent Jesus.*

Faith began to rise. *The emphasis isn't on me in this situation,* I thought, *but on the One who sent me. I am simply His spokesman. I merely release what He's already done. He has finished the work of delivering this little girl; my prayers release the work. I'm only a distributor of what He's already produced. I just get to enforce the victory!*

With new assurance, I informed the people about what I was planning to do. They nodded in recognition as I mentioned the girl. Expressions of intrigue turned to astonishment as they listened to my plans.

Then I prayed.

On a moonlit night in a tiny, remote village in Guatemala, with a handful of people as my audience, my life changed forever.

Jesus came out of hiding. He became alive . . . relevant . . . sufficient . . . available! A "hidden" Jesus emerged from the cobwebs of my theology. A yesterday Jesus became a today and forever Jesus. A Galilee Jesus became a Guatemala Jesus.

And a new plan unfolded to me. A new concept emerged: Jesus and me.

PATTERNS IN HEAVEN

For the first time, I understood the heavenly pattern: Jesus is the Victor—we're the enforcers; Jesus is the Redeemer—we're the releasers; Jesus is the Head—we're the Body.

Yes, He set the little girl free. Yes, the village turned to Christ. Yes, Jesus prevailed through a sent one.

So the partnership goes on—God and humans. But the correct pattern is critical: My *prayers* of intercession release Christ's finished *work* of intercession.

His work empowers my prayers—my prayers release His work.

Mine extends His—His authorizes mine.

Mine activates His—His validates mine.

In GOD, Inc., we're not in the production department; we're in distribution. *BIG* difference. He's the generator. We're the distributors.

UNTYING THOSE WHO ARE BOUND

There are many wounded and hurting individuals "tied to trees" around the world. You go to school with some; others live across the street from you. One of them probably just served you in a check-out line, seated you in a restaurant, or helped you find a DVD. Their chains are alcohol, drugs, abuse, broken dreams, rejection, pornography, money—you get the point.

Plan A is for supernatural but ordinary people like you and me to (1) wholeheartedly believe in the victory of Calvary—to be convinced that it was complete and final and (2) to rise up in our role as sent ones, ambassadors, authorized representatives of the Victor. Our challenge isn't so much to liberate as to believe in the Liberator; it's not so much to heal as to believe in the Healer.

Plan B is to waste the Cross; to leave the tormented in their torment; to scream with our silence, "There is no hope!"; to hear the Father say again, "I looked, but found no one"; to hear the

Son cry once more, "The laborers! Where are the laborers?"

Let's untie some folks. Let's tell them there's a God who cares. Let's represent—let's mediate—let's intercede!

PRAYER IN PRACTICE

Father God, I have to admit, my world is being rocked by what I'm reading. The fact that You've already done the work and are simply waiting for me to pray it through—that blows my mind. Still, I'm so eager to walk with that kind of purpose and authority—not because I want to get the credit for doing amazing things, but because I want to see Your glory and power. Jesus, thank You for opening the way for me. Help me to see those in need around me, and guide me as I simply represent You to a hurting world. Amen.

THINGS THAT MAKE YA GO HMM...

1. What's the difference between intercession and intercessory prayer? Why is this difference important?
2. How are intercession and mediation related?
3. Explain how our *prayers* are an extension of Jesus' *work*.
4. How does it make you feel to know that Jesus always represents you to the Father?
5. Do you know anyone "chained to a tree"? How can you help him or her?

Notes

1. *The Consolidated Webster Encyclopedic Dictionary* (Chicago, IL: Consolidated Book Publishers, 1954), p. 384.
2. Ibid., p. 450.

3. Jack Canfield and Mark Victor Hansen, *Chicken Soup for the Soul* (Deerfield Beach, FL: Health Communications, Inc., 1993), p. 74.

4. R. Arthur Mathews, *Born for Battle* (Robesonia, PA: OMF Books, 1978), p. 106.

MEETINGS: THE GOOD, THE BAD AND THE UGLY

CHAPTER 4

Dutch Sheets, I want you to meet Celia Merchant."

It was 1977, and I was a student in Bible college. I'd just enjoyed a time of private prayer and had emerged from the prayer room to see two individuals carrying a large folding table. One of them was a male friend of mine; the other was the most beautiful young lady I'd ever laid eyes on.

Oh, it wasn't the first time I'd seen her, but it was my first face-to-face encounter. Weak-kneed and tongue-tied, I nearly tripped over myself as I grabbed her end of the table. Being the hero that I am, I relieved her of her burden and practically knocked the other guy off his feet showing how fast I could carry that table.

He then introduced me to what had to be my missing rib, and I knew life would never be right if I didn't marry this woman. I told God as much. Fortunately, He agreed—and so did she. Looking back, I sure am glad I spent that time in prayer. I wouldn't have wanted to miss that *meeting*!

Boy Meets Baseball

I had another memorable *meeting* when I was in the sixth grade. This one wasn't so pleasant, though it would also remain with me for the rest of my life. A baseball *met* my front teeth. The baseball won—they usually do. I have two nice caps on my front teeth today as a result of that *meeting*.

I thought about revealing that I was trying to teach another kid to catch a baseball when it happened, but that would be too embarrassing. I won't mention that I was demonstrating what *not* to do when the accident happened. But I will say that when teaching kids the fine points of baseball, show them what to do—not what not to do. Doing it backward leads to unpleasant *meetings* and cosmetic smiles.

GOD MEETS A MATE, SATAN MEETS HIS MATCH

A figure hangs on a cross between heaven and Earth. Two *meetings* are about to take place: one good and pleasant, one ugly and violent. A Man is about to *meet* His bride and a serpent is about to *meet* a curveball to the teeth:

> For this cause a man shall leave his father and mother, and shall cleave to his wife; and the two shall become one flesh. This mystery is great; but I am speaking with reference to Christ and the church (Eph. 5:31-32).

> Arise, O LORD; save me, O my God! For Thou hast smitten all my enemies on the cheek; Thou hast shattered the teeth of the wicked (Ps. 3:7, *KJV*).

Only God could plan such an event—let alone have it turn out perfectly. Only He could marry such extremes in one occurrence. Who but He could shed blood to create life, use pain to bring healing, allow injustice to satisfy justice and accept rejection to restore acceptance? Who else could use such an evil act to accomplish so much good? Who could transform an act of amazing love into such violence, and vice versa? Only God.

Isn't it fascinating that the serpent, who accomplished his greatest victory from a tree (of the knowledge of good and evil) suffered his greatest defeat from a tree (the Cross of Calvary)?

Don't you find it ironic that the first Adam succumbed to temptation in a garden (Eden) and the last Adam overcame His greatest temptation in a garden (Gethsemane)?

Can God ever write a script!

Perhaps you've guessed by now that hidden somewhere in these three stories—about my wife, the baseball and the Cross—

are pictures of intercession. The Hebrew word for intercession, *paga*, means "to meet."[1] As we've already seen by studying the English word, intercession isn't just a prayer you pray, it's something you do that isn't limited to praying. In fact, *paga* has several meanings that we'll look at throughout this book. But first, let's check out what's behind this "meeting" thing.

IT'S MEETIN' TIME

Intercession creates a *meeting*. Intercessors *meet* with God; they also *meet* the powers of darkness. Why else do you think we have prayer *meetings*?

Similar to Christ's, often our *meeting* with God is to effect another *meeting*—a reconciliation. We *meet* with Him, asking Him to *meet* with someone else. We become the *go-between*: "Heavenly Father, I come to You today (a *meeting*) asking You to touch Scott (another *meeting*)." On the opposite end of the spectrum, as Christ did through spiritual warfare, our *meeting* with the enemy is to undo a *meeting*—a breaking, a severing, a disuniting. All of

RANDOM FACTS ABOUT MEETINGS

Did ya know . . .

- 11 million meetings are held each day.
- The average professional worker attends 61.8 meetings each month.[2]
- 50 percent of those meetings are a waste of time![3]
- 91 percent of all meeting attendees daydream, and almost 40 percent have actually dozed off during a meeting.[4]

our intercession will involve one or both of these facets: reconciling or breaking, uniting or disuniting.

Sometimes when God *meets* with people, the miraculous happens. In 1980, I was on another of my many journeys into Guatemala. On one occasion, my wife and I and another couple were ministering to an elderly lady who had recently been saved. Approximately six months earlier this lady had fallen from a stool and severely broken her ankle. The fracture wasn't healing well; her ankle was still badly swollen and she was in a lot of pain. While we visited with her, the other gentleman and I both sensed that God wanted to heal her ankle—right then.

After sharing this with her and asking her permission, we instructed her to prop her leg on a stool. I began to pray . . . sort of.

Has God ever interrupted you? He did that to me on this occasion. (Not that I ever mind when He does that.) When I stepped *between* her and God to effect a *meeting*, the presence of God came so powerfully into the room that I stopped in mid-stride and mid-sentence. I'd taken one step toward her and uttered one word: "Father."

That's all He needed!

It's as though He was so eager to touch this dear lady that He couldn't wait any longer. I realize that what I'm about to say may sound overly dramatic, but it's exactly what took place. The presence of the Holy Spirit filled the room so strongly that I froze in my tracks, stopped speaking and began to weep. My wife and the other couple also began to weep. And the lady we were ministering to followed suit. Her foot began to bounce up and down on the stool, shaking uncontrollably for several minutes as she had a powerful encounter with the Holy Spirit—a *meeting*! The Lord healed her and filled her with His Spirit.

Group Meetings

On the same visit to Guatemala, my wife and I, along with the couple previously mentioned, were asked to pray for a woman hospitalized with tuberculosis. We found her in a ward with approximately 40 other women; the beds were only about three feet apart. It was simply an area in the hospital where the doctors and nurses could attend the very poor. There weren't even partitions to separate the women. And yes, this woman was coughing her tuberculosis all over those around her.

As we talked and prayed with her, we noticed the lady in the next bed observing us closely. When we finished, she asked if we'd be willing to pray for her. After asking about her need, she pulled her arms out from under the covers and showed us her two hands, curled back toward her body, somewhat frozen in that position. They were totally unusable. Her feet were the same way. While in the hospital for back surgery, the doctor had accidentally cut a nerve in her spinal cord, leaving her in this condition. There was nothing they could do to correct the problem.

We were filled with compassion and asked the Lord to *meet* her need. Nothing noticeable happened, but we encouraged her to trust the Lord and drifted across the room to see if we could share Jesus with anyone else.

Just as we began to visit with another lady across the room, we heard a sudden commotion and someone screaming, "*Milagro! Milagro! Milagro!*" We turned to look and saw the lady moving her hands wildly, opening and closing them, wiggling her fingers, kicking her feet under the covers and shouting the Spanish word for "miracle." A *meeting* had taken place!

I don't know who was more surprised—the lady who was healed, the other ladies in the room, or me. I hoped for a miracle, but I don't think I believed for one. I remember thinking, *This sort of thing only happened during Bible days.*

The next thing we knew, every woman in the room was begging us to minister to them. We went from bed to bed—just like we knew what we were doing—leading women to Christ and praying for their recoveries. I remember thinking, *This is wild. Is this real or am I dreaming? We're having revival in a hospital ward!* Several were saved. The lady with tuberculosis was also healed and another lady who had been scheduled for exploratory surgery the following morning was instead sent home healed.

What on Earth can turn a sad, hopeless, disease-filled ward into a church service? God! God *meeting* with people. And prayer *meetings* create God *meetings*!

She-Bear Meetings

I don't want to mislead you into thinking that miracles will always happen as easily as they did on these two occasions. You've probably already experienced the disappointment of praying for someone's healing and not seeing any changes. Whatever the results, however, it's key that we realize what we're doing in the spirit realm. Through intercession—whether it lasts days or minutes—we can bring individuals into a one-on-one meeting with God. And that's the important thing.

There's another kind of intercession that's just as significant, one that causes just as much in-your-face contact. I call this "the bear anointing" because of Proverbs 17:12, which reads: "Let a man *meet* a bear robbed of her cubs, rather than a fool in his folly" (emphasis added).

I've never met a she-bear in the wild with or without her cubs, and I hope I never do. But a wise old woodsman who was instructing me in the art of surviving bear encounters gave me the following piece of wisdom: "Son, try to avoid them, if possible. But if you can't, and it's a female you run into, don't ever get between mama and her cubs. Because if you do, there's fixin' to be a *meeting*, and you're gonna be on the receiving end!"

Obviously, Proverbs 17:12 isn't talking about prayer. My point is that meetings can be unpleasant—sometimes downright ugly! In other words, consider yourself warned: Intercession can be violent!

Do you remember the meeting Satan had with Jesus at Calvary when Christ interceded for us? Satan had come between God and His "cubs." Bad move. Satan's worst nightmare came true when, with 4,000 years of pent-up fury, Jesus *met* him at Calvary. The earth rocked—and I do mean literally—with the force of the battle (see Matt. 27:51). The very sun grew dark as the war raged (see v. 45). At the moment when Satan thought he was having his greatest triumph, he and all his forces heard the most terrifying sound they'd ever heard: God's mocking laugh (see Ps. 2:4).

Meanwhile, the behind-the-scene action was violent. Captives were rescued (see 1 Pet. 3:19; 4:6; Isa. 61:1); bruises were inflicted (see Gen. 3:15; Isa. 53:5; 1 Pet. 2:24); keys were exchanged, authority was transferred (see Matt. 28:18).

An interesting word is used in 1 John 3:8 (*KJV*) that adds insight to what happened at the cross. The verse reads, "For this purpose the Son of God was manifested, that he might destroy the works of the devil." "Destroy" is the Greek word *luo*, which has both a legal and a physical meaning. The legal meaning of *luo* is (1) to pronounce or determine that something or someone is no longer bound, and (2) to dissolve or void a contract or anything that legally binds.[5] Jesus came to dissolve the legal hold Satan had over us and to pronounce that we were no longer bound by his works. He "voided the contract," breaking Satan's dominion over us.

The physical meaning of *luo* is "to dissolve or melt, break, beat something to pieces or untie something that is bound."[6] In Acts 27:41, the boat Paul traveled on was broken to pieces (*luo*) by the force of a storm. In 2 Peter 3:10,12, we're told that one day the elements of the earth will melt or dissolve (*luo*) from a great heat. So Jesus not only delivered us legally, but He also destroyed the opposition's hold—which brought healing, set captives free, lifted oppression and liberated those under demonic control.

ENFORCING THE VICTORY

Does this mean the job's completely done? Nope. Otherwise we wouldn't encounter the ongoing attacks of the enemy. Our job is to enforce the victory as we also *meet* the powers of darkness. Although Jesus fully accomplished the task of breaking the authority of Satan and voiding his legal hold upon the human race once and for all, someone on Earth must represent Him in that victory and enforce it.

With this in mind and remembering that the Hebrew word for intercession, *paga*, means *to meet*, let's state it this way: We, through *prayers* of intercession, *meet* the powers of darkness, enforcing the victory Christ accomplished when He *met* them in His *work* of intercession.

A *meeting* can be a good and pleasant experience or it can be a violent confrontation between opposing forces. The intercessor is either going to *meet* with God for the purpose of reconciling the world to the Father and His wonderful blessings, or he

"I will give you the keys of the kingdom of heaven; and whatever you shall bind on earth shall be bound in heaven, and whatever you shall loose [*luo*] on earth shall be loosed [*luo*] in heaven." —Matthew 16:19

is going to *meet* satanic forces of opposition to enforce the victory of Calvary. The purpose will vary, but one thing's certain: The prayers of an understanding intercessor WILL create a *meeting*. And when the *meeting* comes to a close, something will have changed.

Don't be intimidated by the size of the giant. And don't believe it when others say you can't do this because you're too young or your past is too checkered with mistakes. Jesus has qualified you to represent Him. Be like the small boy playing in the backyard with his bat and ball:

"I'm the greatest baseball player in the world," he said proudly. Then he tossed the ball in the air, swung and missed. Undaunted, he picked up the ball, threw it into the air and said to himself, "I'm the greatest player ever!" He swung at the ball, and again he missed. He paused a moment to examine bat and ball carefully. Then once again he threw the ball into the air and said, "I'm the greatest baseball player who ever lived." He swung the bat hard and again missed the ball.

"Wow!" he exclaimed. "What a pitcher!"[7]

When it comes to intercession, don't believe the unbelief. You *can* do it!

PRAYER IN PRACTICE

Lord, I'm amazed by Your gift of intercession. Thank You for even allowing me to have a role in effecting and enforcing Your victory here on Earth. I praise You, Jesus, for what You did on the cross and how it sealed the fate of Satan. Father, thank You for Your jealousy over me. I pray that I'll see more miraculous meetings between You and the people I pray for. Now give me the wisdom to know when to meet with You and when to "meet" with the forces of evil. Help me as I learn more about the power of intercession. Amen.

THINGS THAT MAKE YA GO HMM...

1. Name the two opposite kinds of meetings you can encounter in intercession. What does each do?
2. Think of someone you know who needs a meeting with God. How and when can you help facilitate this?
3. In what areas of your life do you need to remind Satan of Jesus' victory?
4. Have you ever been in a setting where God came and met with the group? Describe the experience.

Notes

1. Francis Brown, S. R. Driver, and Charles A. Briggs, *The New Brown-Driver, Briggs-Gesenius Hebrew and English Lexicon* (Peabody, MA: Hendrickson Publishers, 1979), p. 803.
2. A network MCI Conferencing White Paper: *Meetings in America: A study of trends, costs and attitudes toward business travel, teleconferencing, and their impact on productivity* (Greenwich, CT: INFOCOMM, 1998), p. 3.
3. Robert B. Nelson and Peter Economy, *Better Business Meetings* (Burr Ridge, IL: Irwin Inc, 1995), p. 5.
4. *Meetings in America*, p. 10.
5. Spiros Zodhiates, *Hebrew-Greek Key Study Bible—New American Standard* (Chattanooga, TN: AMG Publishers, 1984; revised edition, 1990), p. 1583.
6. Ibid.
7. Jack Canfield and Mark Victor Hansen, *Chicken Soup for the Soul* (Deerfield Beach, FL: Health Communications, Inc., 1993), p. 74.

I GET BY WITH A LITTLE HELP FROM MY FRIENDS

CHAPTER 5

There's a story about baseball great Jackie Robinson that goes like this:

> Jackie Robinson was the first black to play major league baseball. While breaking baseball's color barrier, he faced jeering crowds in every stadium. While playing one day in his home stadium in Brooklyn, he committed an error. His own fans began to ridicule him. He stood at second base, humiliated, while the fans jeered. Then shortstop "Pee Wee" Reese came over and stood next to him. He put his arm around Jackie Robinson and faced the crowd. The fans grew quiet. Robinson later said that arm around his shoulder saved his career.[1]

Everyone needs a friend like "Pee Wee"—someone who will put an arm around you when you need support, encouragement or relief. It's a powerful thing when someone comes alongside you to simply *be* with you at your lowest point. And if we want to be just as good a friend, we'll return the favor. The Bible says that we are to "weep with those who weep" (Rom. 12:15) and to "bear one another's burdens" (Gal. 6:2). But while those verses involve sharing each other's pain, there's more to the picture. We're not simply to *carry* burdens for our brothers and sisters in Christ; we're to *carry them away*. There's a big difference! One involves sharing a load; the other involves removing a load.

The New Testament actually uses two words for "bearing." The first word, *anechomai*, means "to sustain, bear or hold up against a thing,"[2] just like when you tie a stake to a tomato plant to sustain it from the weight it carries. The strength of the stake is transferred to the plant and bears it up. You've probably heard the verses in Colossians 3:13 and Ephesians 4:2 that tell us to "bear with one another." Paul's not just suggesting, "OK, would you mind putting up with one another until I get back?" He's commanding us to "stake yourselves to one another." In other words, we're to come alongside a weak brother or sister who's weighed down, and say, "I'm not going to let you fall and be broken or destroyed. I'm staking myself to you, through thick and thin. My strength is now yours. Go ahead, lean on me. As long as I can stand, you will, too."

SEND THAT THING HOME!

The second word for "bearing" is *bastazo* and means "to bear, lift or carry" something with the idea of carrying it *away* or to *remove* it.[3] *Bastazo* is used in the following verses:

> Now we who are strong ought to *bear* the weaknesses of those without strength and not just please ourselves. Let each of us please his neighbor for his good, to his edification. For even Christ did not please Himself; but as it is written, "The reproaches of those who reproached Thee fell upon Me" (Rom. 15:1-3, emphasis added).

> *Bear* one another's burdens, and thus fulfill the law of Christ (Gal. 6:2, emphasis added).

Christ interceded for us on the cross by carrying away our sins. Notice that He didn't just carry our burdens *for* us; He carried them *away from* us. We're to do the same thing for others. But there's an important thing to remember: We're not literally *re-doing* what Christ did; we're *re-presenting* what He did. There's a big difference between the two. We're representing Him, extending His work. *He* does the healing, is the life, the comfort, the power. We just extend and apply those things.

Even cooler is that He's "made us able ministers of the new testament" (2 Cor. 3:6, *KJV*). What does that mean? It means that you're fully capable of extending the blessings and provisions that are contained in the new covenant ("testament" is just a *KJV* word for "covenant") that Jesus established. Just as I stated in the last chapter, it doesn't matter how old you are or what kind of experiences you've been through; Christ has made you an "able minister."

YOU'RE NOT A LONE RANGER

This principle of bearing another's burden and carrying it away came alive for me through my friend Mike Anderson. He and his wife were missionaries in Jamaica and were in the midst of a life-and-death struggle with their two-year-old son, who had contracted a critical illness. The boy's health had gotten so bad that

RANDOM WAYS YOU CAN MINISTER

· Offer to tutor someone who's struggling with his or her schoolwork.
· Make (or buy) an extra lunch each week for someone who's often made fun of at school.
· Mow your neighbor's yard for free.
· Be the first person to befriend a new kid at your school or youth group.
· Write an unsigned letter of encouragement to someone in need (maybe even a teacher).
· Devote a Saturday to helping a widow at your church with house-maintenance projects.
· Pray for your enemies.

he was near death. That's when Mike called me and a few other individuals in the United States.

"I desperately need your help, Dutch," Mike said.

"What is it?" I asked.

"It's my son, Toby. He's deathly ill with a raging fever. The doctors haven't been able to find the cause. They've done all they know to do, but nothing seems to help. They even doubt whether he'll survive another night in his condition. I've been praying and praying for him but can't seem to break this attack. While I was praying, the Lord showed me that Toby's condition is caused by a strong spirit of infirmity. But after warring against it for hours, I still haven't been able to break its power over my son. But I feel that the Lord has shown me that if some strong intercessors join me, we can break this attack."

Now understand this: Mike and his wife, Pam, are strong in the Lord. They pray. They have faith. They understand authority and spiritual warfare and all the other things related to intercession. And they weren't walking in sin. So why couldn't they get the breakthrough they needed on their own?

I don't know. But I suspect the Lord wanted to teach them (and those of us praying with them) the principle I'm now sharing with you.

The people I was meeting with, and a few others Mike had called, went into prayer. We asked God to meet (*paga*) with this child. We basically said, "Father, allow us to move into our priestly role as intercessors (*paga*), enforcing the victory of Jesus in this situation, re-presenting or administering the blessings of the new covenant. Stake us to Toby and allow us, along with Christ, to be touched with the feeling of this infirmity. Lay on (*paga*) us this burden that we might bear (*nasa, bastazo*) it away. We ask this in Jesus' name, based on who He is and what He has done."

Then we bound the power of Satan over this child's life—in Christ's name, of course, because it was His victory we were

"administering." (See, this isn't just some meaningless religious rit-
ual we Christians do at the end of each prayer. There's a reason
behind it.) Then we growled with "the bear anointing" (see chapter
4). OK, so I'm kidding—we didn't really. But I swear I heard a growl
in the Spirit! Or maybe it was a roar—the Lord does "roar out of
Zion," you know (see Joel 3:16; Amos 1:2). And we're pretty certain
He did, because Mike called back a few hours later with the good
news: "Almost immediately after I contacted several of you to pray
with me, the fever broke and Toby began to improve. Within a few
hours he was well and was released from the hospital."

Praise God! The Body of Christ had functioned as the Lord
intended, and Jesus was glorified.

But Mike had more. "I asked the Lord why I needed others
to help me break this attack against my son. He reminded me of
the story of Joshua and the army of Israel coming to the aid of the
Gibeonites, who were helplessly outnumbered by five armies."
Mike then recounted the story from Joshua 9 and 10 for me.

The Gibeonites were one of the Canaanite tribes that Joshua
and Israel were supposed to destroy. But the Gibeonites were
sneaky; they tricked the Israelites by pretending to be from a far-
away country so that the Israelites would enter into a covenant
with them. Instead of praying about it first, Joshua and the
Israelites jumped into a long-term agreement. (Ever "forgotten"
to pray about something and gotten into trouble? Not a good idea.)

Even though it was birthed out of a scam, the covenant was
still valid and made Israel an ally of Gibeon. So a few days later,
when five armies marched against Gibeon, they called upon
Joshua for help—knowing the covenant required the Israelites
to help out. Sure enough, Joshua and his army traveled all night
to arrive in time and rescue the Gibeonites. The entire story is an
incredible demonstration of the power of covenant.

After reminding Mike of that story, the Lord planted the following thought in his heart as to why he needed help from others

to overcome this spirit: *Sometimes the covenant of the Lord is released to you through others coming to your aid!*

Isn't that crazy? The Almighty administers the blessings of the covenant when we rush to help our friends in their time of need. That's what intercession is all about. *Paga*: He "lays on" us someone else's need. *Anechomai*: We "stake" ourselves to that person. *Bastazo*: We "carry away" the weakness or burden.

THIS MEANS WAR!

At times you'll find that when Christ lays a prayer mission or burden on you (*paga*) so that you can bear it away (*nasa, bastazo*), the task involves warfare. The truth is, you can't separate the word "intercession" (*paga*) from the concept of warfare. (We'll find out more about this in upcoming chapters.)

Both the Hebrew and Greek words used for "tread," *darak* (Hebrew)[4] and *pateo* (Greek),[5] involve the concept of violence or war. In fact, *darak* is associated with "bending the bow"[6] when an

NAME THAT TUNE

He is trampling out the vintage where the grapes of wrath are stored/He has loosed the fateful lightning of His terrible swift sword.[7]

Recognize that verse from a famous song? It's from "The Battle Hymn of the Republic," one of America's most patriotic songs. But the songwriter didn't have to look too far to find the lyrics—they're from Revelation 19:15: "And from His mouth comes a sharp sword, so that with it He may smite the nations; and He will rule them with a rod of iron; and He treads the wine press of the fierce wrath of God, the Almighty."

arrow is about to be shot, and it's still used today in Israel for the command, "Load your weapons." Both words are used when referring to treading or trampling in a wine press, which is fittingly symbolic of Christ overcoming His enemies, recorded in Isaiah 63:3 and Revelation 19:15.

What's amazing is that these same two words—*darak* and *pateo*—aren't just used to describe Christ at war; they reference *our* warfare. In Joshua 1:3, the Lord said to Joshua, "Every place on which the sole of your foot treads, I have given it to you, just as I spoke to Moses." The word "tread," of course, is *darak*. God wasn't telling Israel that everywhere they walked or stepped was theirs. He'd already marked off the perimeters of the inheritance. He was saying symbolically, "Every place that you're willing to load your weapons and take, I'm going to give to you."

With that comes a deeper question: Was God giving, or were they taking? When we engage in warfare, does Jesus fight for us or do we just claim the victory? The answer is YES! Remember the Israelites under Moses? They wouldn't load their weapons and fight—they were afraid and wouldn't *darak*. As a result, God wouldn't give the land to them. It took a Joshua generation to stand up to the enemies and wage war—and claim the land.

Don't think for a moment that it's any different for us today. These things happened to Israel as types or shadows for us (see 1 Cor. 10:6,11). Joshua was a representative of Jesus. Not until the people were completely surrendered to the will of Joshua (which was the will of God the Father) could they possess the land. The same goes for you and me. As long as we're ready to take up our weapons and become sold-out to the commands of our leader, Jesus, then He's ready to give us whatever territory we tread. It doesn't automatically come just because we belong to Him; we have to take "the weapons of our warfare" (2 Cor. 10:4) and *darak!*

This is intercession, just as it was through Christ and is through us. Sometimes it's a matter of holding up another person. Other times it's stepping in and removing that person's burden. And often it's waging war on darkness and declaring the victory Jesus has already won. My prayer is that your generation—often called the Joshua generation—will understand all three of these elements of intercession and refuse to wander around a desert aimlessly like Moses' people did. It's time to declare war! It's time to take the land!

PRAYER IN PRACTICE

Mighty God, You have won the battle. You've defeated the powers of darkness. I praise You for Your victory. Thank You for allowing me to share in the win and to claim back what the enemy has stolen. Help me to daily pick up my weapons. Help me to know when to come alongside others and strengthen them in places where they're weak. Jesus, help me to understand Your power that removes their burdens. I trust You to guide me. Amen.

THINGS THAT MAKE YA GO HMM ...

1. How have you staked yourself to someone in prayer? What was the outcome?
2. Do we do the bearing away of someone else's burden or does Christ? Explain.
3. What does God ask us to do when waging war on the enemy?
4. What role can others sometimes play in the Lord's releasing His covenant of blessings in your life?
5. What held the Moses-led Israelites back from taking the land that was promised to them?

Notes

1. Craig Brian Larson, *Illustrations for Preaching and Teaching* (Grand Rapids, MI: Baker Book House, 1993), p. 144.
2. Joseph Henry Thayer, *A Greek-English Lexicon of the New Testament* (Grand Rapids, MI: Baker Book House, 1977), p. 45.
3. Ibid., p. 99.
4. R. Laird Harris, Gleason L. Archer, Jr., and Bruce K. Waltke, *Theological Wordbook of the Old Testament* (Chicago, IL: Moody Press, 1980; Grand Rapids, MI: William B. Eerdmans Publishing Co., revised edition, 1991), p. 453.
5. Spiros Zodhiates, *The Complete Word Study Dictionary* (Iowa Falls, IA: Word Bible Publishers, 1992), p. 1128.
6. Harris, Archer, Waltke, *Theological Wordbook of the Old Testament*, p. 453.
7. Words by Julia Ward Howe, "The Battle Hymn of the Republic," melody attributed to William Steffe.

NO TRESPASSING

CHAPTER 6

No dumping allowed. Trespassers will be violated.

I used to laugh every time I drove by that sign. It wasn't a homemade sign. It was a professionally made metal sign posted by a city in Oklahoma. It was even the fancy kind with fluorescent letters that could be easily seen at night. But the people who made it had worded it incorrectly. Instead of saying, "Trespassers (or Violators) will be prosecuted," they worded it, "Trespassers will be violated."

I hope they were simply confused. Perhaps they weren't. Maybe in that town the law violated trespassers instead of prosecuting them—but that sounds a little icky to me. Either way, it was obvious that those townspeople were serious about their property.

As Christians, we've been given property from God Himself. And to keep out unwanted visitors, we can establish protective boundaries. (No, not for using against your younger brother—I'm talking about spiritual intruders.) In a way, we have the right to stake our own warning signs in the spirit: "No dumping allowed, Satan. Trespassers will be violated." The Bible contains specific instructions on how we can set up these boundary markers.

In Joshua 19, the Hebrew word for intercession, *paga*, is used several times. The passage describes the dimensions or boundaries of each of the tribes of Israel. *Paga* is translated several ways in different translations, including "reached to," "touched," "bordered," "boundary." The *Spirit-Filled Bible* says that *paga*, as used in this context, is the extent to which a boundary reaches.[1]

It seems kind of weird that the same word for "intercession" is used to describe the details for marking out Israel's land. And yet it's not just coincidence that the concepts of prayer and protection are linked through the same word. God intended for us to establish boundaries of safety in each of our lives. You can build these boundaries around yourself and others through your own intercession. It's important to understand, however, that protection isn't an automatic thing just because you're a Christian. We must do things to secure it, one of which is building boundaries (*paga*) of protection through prayer.

DWELLING IN THE SECRET PLACE

Consistency is a key when it comes to prayer for protection. Psalm 91:1 (*NKJV*) says, "He who dwells in the secret place of the most High shall abide under the shadow of the Almighty." That means that when we "dwell" close to God, we "abide" under His protective shadow. We camp out there. We move next door to Him. We set up residence in His district. And the result is having the Great Defender as your personal bodyguard.

But this doesn't come through a casual relationship with God. The word "dwell" in Psalm 91:1 is *yashab*, which means "to remain or abide; to dwell in or inhabit."[2] And the word "abide" is *luwn*, which means, among other things, "to spend the night."[3] Using these definitions, let's restate the verse: "He that *inhabits* the secret place of the most High shall *spend the night* under the shadow of the Almighty."

Jesus equated "the secret place" to our prayer closet (see Matt. 6:6). So if you're expecting to have God's divine protection, you'll find it on your knees. But prayer must be a lifestyle, not a once-in-a-blue-moon activity. It's like the Word of God; we don't read enough today for the entire week. We have to get our "daily bread," or manna. Likewise, we must go to the secret place daily, and when we do, we can "spend the night" there. The next morning, we get up and go there again to meet our needs for that day. Consistency is a key.

Where's your secret place? Is it close to God, or are you not even in the same zip code? You can't expect to have solid walls of protection without a prayer life that's built on being close to Him every day.

PRAY—NOW!!!

Ever heard someone talk about doing something "at the perfect time"? When we're in need of encouragement and a friend happens to say something that lifts our spirits, we say that he or she came "at just the right time."

We can be at the perfect time when it comes to prayer, too—especially in praying for protection. Don't you think that when that bomb landed on the ship's deck (see story below) that those World War II sailors needed protection at just the right time? The same goes for you, your family, your friends, etc. There are *specific* times when the Holy Spirit will alert us to particular situations that need protective prayer. These are what the Scriptures call *kairos* times.

There are two Greek words for "time." One is *chronos*, which is time in general; it's basically the "time in which anything *is* done." The other word, *kairos*, is the strategic or "right time—the

SHELTER FROM THE STORM

A minister served on a ship during World War II. Every day he and a few other sailors would have a prayer time, seeking God for protection for themselves and the ship. What were they doing? Building boundaries (*paga*) of protection.

"In one battle," he says, "an enemy plane dropped a bomb onto the deck of our ship. Instead of exploding, however, to everyone's astonishment the bomb bounced off the deck and into the water, just like a rubber ball would!" In battle after battle they and the ship were miraculously spared.

opportune point of time at which something *should be* done."[4]

A window of opportunity would be *kairos* time.

A well-timed attack in war would be *kairos* time.

When someone's in danger or about to be attacked by Satan, that's a *kairos* time.

The time of day would be *chronos* time.

In Ephesians 6:18, the apostle Paul says that we are to "pray at all [*kairos*] times in the Spirit" and "be on the alert . . . for all the saints." You've probably heard or read that verse before and thought, *How in the world can I pray nonstop?* Paul isn't telling us here to pray all the time, which would be *chronos*, but to pray at all strategic times (*kairos*). This distinction is even more evident considering that the context of the verse is all about spiritual warfare. We're in a war. If we're alert, the Lord will warn us of the well-timed attacks (*kairos*) of the enemy so that we can create a boundary (*paga*) of protection by praying.

KAIROS—A TIME TO PAGA

As I was praying one morning several years ago, the Lord gave me a mental picture of a rattlesnake coiled at my dad's feet. Seemed a little weird at the time, but it also seemed like a *kairos* time to me! I spent about 15 minutes praying earnestly for Dad's protection until I felt released from the urgency.

The next day he called me—he was in Florida, I was in Texas—and said, "You'll never guess what happened yesterday. Jodie [my stepmother] went out back to the shed. Before walking in like she normally would, she pushed the door open, stopped and looked down. There where she was about to step was a coiled rattlesnake. She backed away carefully, came and got me, and I killed it."

What was I doing as I prayed for him? Setting boundaries (*paga*) of protection around him and Jodie. How did I pray? I asked the Father to protect them. I bound any attempt of Satan to harm them. I quoted a verse or two of Scripture promising protection. Then I prayed in the Spirit.

You might argue that God didn't need me to pray for 15 minutes to protect them from a rattlesnake. And you know what? You're right. God didn't "need" seven days of marching around Jericho to tear it down either, but He chose to do it that way. He doesn't "need" to spit in a person's eye to heal them, but He did that once. (Don't believe me? Check out Mark 8:22-26.) Why He requires things to be done certain ways we don't always know; but we do know that for us *obedience is the key*. If He says that it takes 15 minutes or 3 hours or 3 months, then that's exactly what it will take.

THE NICK OF TIME

I had a friend in Dallas several years ago who experienced an interesting answer to prayer in a *kairos* situation. She'd gone

HEADS UP!

The Bible speaks of well-timed (*kairos*) temptations (see Luke 4:13; 8:13). Obviously, not every temptation is particular to a time, but Satan certainly targets us with specific things at specific times. Haven't you noticed how temptations always seem to come on strongest when you're the weakest? It pays to be alert, both for ourselves and for others. That's why it's so important that we lift others up in prayer when we know they're going through a rough time. Find yourself a group of friends to whom you can be accountable and agree to lift each other up daily—even hourly—in prayer. When you're about to give in to a temptation, call or IM a buddy and have him or her pray with you.

early one morning to visit her son and daughter-in-law. The son worked an all-night shift, so the mom visited with his wife for a while. But as time wore on and the son didn't arrive, Mom began to feel uneasy. Something didn't seem right.

Thinking that perhaps he was still at work, they called his place of employment. "No," they were told, "he's already left."

Becoming more worried, the mother suggested they get in the car and head toward his workplace. As she and her daughter-in-law drove on a busy Dallas parkway, they saw him coming from the other direction on his motorcycle, traveling around 40 to 50 miles per hour. To their horror, they watched as he fell asleep and veered off the road, hit the curb and flew 40 to 50 feet through the air. He wasn't even wearing a helmet.

As her son was moving through the air, the mom prayed, "*Jesus, protect my son!*" She continued to pray as they turned around and drove back to him. A crowd had already gathered around him when they arrived on the scene wondering what they would find.

They found a miracle! No injuries. No bones broken, no lacerations, no internal injuries—just a dazed young man wondering what had happened.

Paga happened . . . *kairos paga* happened! Boundaries happened. A mother picked up on the warning from the Holy Spirit and was in the right place at the right time to protect her son.

Does this mean that if you weren't there praying when someone you love had an accident, then you're to blame for their injury or death? Of course not. If we all played that guessing game, it would drive us insane. It simply means that we must be alert; and when warnings do come from the Holy Spirit, we must respond by praying (building some boundaries).

Establishing Life-Saving Boundaries

Perhaps the most amazing example of *kairos*-timed intercession in my life happened on another of my journeys to Guatemala. I was one of 40 to 45 individuals traveling to a remote place on the Passion River in the Peten Jungle. Our mission was to build a combination clinic and outreach station on the river. We would construct two buildings as well as do a little preaching in the nearby villages.

It was an amazing trip. We ate monkey meat and boa constrictor. We killed huge tarantulas, a nine-inch scorpion and a coral snake in our camp. I was attacked by ants that, unbeknownst to us, had taken refuge in the lumber we were hauling (and sleeping on) as we traveled all night up the river. We flew in old, rickety army planes and landed on fields from which goats had to be cleared prior to our arrival. (None of this has anything to do with prayer, but doesn't it show you how incredibly brave I am and how much I've suffered for the cause of Christ?!)

Prior to leaving for the jungle, we spent our first night (Friday) in Guatemala City, the capital of Guatemala. We'd arranged months earlier for the Guatemalan airlines to fly us the following day into the jungle. On our arrival at the airport Saturday afternoon, we were informed that they'd changed their plans and would fly us to our destination not that day but the next.

Our leaders felt an urgency to go as scheduled because of the limited amount of time to accomplish our mission, so they pressed the airlines to honor their original agreement.

"No," the manager said in his broken English, "we take you tomorrow."

"But you agreed months ago to take us today," we argued.

"No pilot available," they countered.

"Find one," we pleaded.

"What's your hurry? Enjoy the city," they said.

And so it went for three hours, in and out of offices, meeting with one official, then another. Finally, in exasperation, one of them threw up his hands and said, "OK, we take you now! Get on that plane—quickly!"

We all ran to the plane, throwing our bags and tools into the baggage area ourselves. We wanted to leave before they changed their minds.

That night, while we were 250 miles away, an earthquake hit Guatemala City and killed 30,000 people in 34 seconds! Had we stayed in the city one more night—as the airlines wanted us to—some of our team would've been killed and others injured. We know this for certain because on our return to the city we saw the building we'd stayed in the night before the earthquake—and would've been staying in again had we not left on Saturday—with huge beams lying across the beds.

The connection between all this and prayer is that an intercessor from our home church back in Ohio had received a strong burden to pray for us on the second day of our journey. For *three hours* she was in intense intercession for us. Can you guess which three hours? Yep, the three hours during which our leaders were negotiating with the airline officials.

We didn't know that our lives were in jeopardy had we stayed another night in Guatemala City, but God did. This intercessor didn't know it either. She only knew that for some reason, she had a strong burden to pray for us. She was alert, as Ephesians 6:18 instructs us to be, and perceived the *kairos* time. There isn't a doubt in my mind that she helped create the protection and intervention we experienced.

There is a life in the secret place, but it's not automatic for believers. Although we are promised protection from our enemy, we have a definite part to play in the securing of it for ourselves and for others. As we grow in intercession, it becomes clear that we can each post a sign for all the forces of hell to see: "Under the Shadow of the Most High. Keep Out!"

PRAYER IN PRACTICE

Father God, I praise You for all the seen and unseen ways
You protect me. Thank You for raising up parents, friends,
teachers and others who pray for me on a regular basis.
Help me to do the same for them. Let me recognize the kairos
times when my prayers are urgently needed. And thank
You for calling me to Your side, to dwell under the shadow
of the Most High. Keep me close to You. Amen.

THINGS THAT MAKE YA GO HMM...

1. In your own words, explain the connection between *paga* and protection.
2. Why isn't protection an automatic thing for Christians? What does that mean for you?
3. What are some ways that you can establish spiritual boundaries of protection in your life?
4. Explain the difference between *chronos* and *kairos* and how this difference relates to intercession.
5. What are some areas of your life where you need to put up a "No Trespassing" sign?

Notes

1. *The Spirit-Filled Bible* (Nashville, TN: Thomas Nelson Publishers, 1991), p. 1097.
2. James Strong, *The New Strong's Exhaustive Concordance of the Bible* (Nashville, TN: Thomas Nelson Publishers, 1990), ref. no. 3427.
3. Francis Brown, S. R. Driver, and Charles A. Briggs, *The New Brown-Driver, Briggs-Gesenius Hebrew and English Lexicon* (Peabody, MA: Hendrickson Publishers, 1979), p. 533.
4. Ethelbert W. Bullinger, *A Critical Lexicon and Concordance to the English and Greek New Testament* (Grand Rapids, MI: Zondervan Publishing House, 1975), p. 804.

BUTTERFLIES, MICE, ELEPHANTS AND BULL'S-EYES

CHAPTER 7

I recently traveled to all 50 states with my friend the prophet Chuck Pierce. No, it wasn't just a nice extended sightseeing trip. Our mission, as given to both of us by God, was to pray for revival in America. While we were in Texas, I spoke at a church and said something that ignited a prophetic flame in Chuck. He ran to the platform, had the nerve to *interrupt* my awesome message, and suddenly began to prophesy. The gist of his words went something like this: "If you'll pray right now, Saddam Hussein will be captured within a week."

This was early in the war in Iraq, when Saddam was still on the run from U.S. forces. He'd been a hunted man for months, yet things were looking pretty bleak as far as tracking him down. So as soon as Chuck had stepped out on a limb with his prophecy, he turned to me with an "I can't believe I just said that" expression on his face, handed me the microphone with a "Well, do something" look in his eyes, and promptly walked off.

I could've killed him. *You do something!* I thought. *You got us into this mess!* But being the faith-filled man of God that I am, I simply cried out to the Lord in my heart, "HELP!!!"

As panic left and self-control returned, I really did look inwardly and asked the Holy Spirit what I should do. Immediately, I felt an impression: *Pray that the witchcraft keeping him hidden be broken.* And so I did just that. As we began to pray, I sensed the need for some servicemen in attendance to also press in with our intercession, so a few came up to do exactly that. We prayed for one soldier from the 4th Infantry and asked God to anoint his division with supernatural ability to do their job in Iraq. As this was occurring, many of the 1,500 to 2,000 people in attendance joined in by praying in the Spirit.

Three days later, the 4th Infantry pulled Saddam from a hole in the ground!

ON THE SPOT

Ever been in a similar situation? OK, you've probably never been in front of 2,000 people when someone went out on a limb—and left you hanging—like Chuck did to me with his radical prophecy of Saddam's capture. But there are times when all of us are confronted with someone or something that we don't know how to pray for. Often we're at a complete loss for words. Other times, we may feel a burden from the Holy Spirit to pray for someone, yet we're clueless as to why—it's just one of those gut-feeling things. In Romans 8:26, Paul gives us some insight as to what we can do during those times: "In the same way, the Spirit helps us in our weakness. We do not know what we ought to pray for, but the Spirit himself intercedes for us with groans that words cannot express."

BEING AT THE RIGHT PLACE AT THE RIGHT TIME

It's OK to not always know how to pray. It's OK to not always have the right words or the instant solution. In fact, the more you grow in God, the more you'll find yourself in prayer situations where you know nothing! The good news: That's the *best* time for the Holy Spirit to take over and guide your prayers.

The perfect example of this is found in Genesis 28:10-17. It's the story of Jacob fleeing from his older brother, Esau. Remember how Jacob gypped Esau into giving him his birthright? Once Big Bro found out what really went down, Jacob was on the run. After

"In prayer, it is better to have heart without words than words without heart." —John Bunyan

traveling all day, he needed a place to spend the night "because the sun was set." Verse 11 says he "lighted upon" (*KJV*) a particular place and there he spent the night. This is another time the word *paga* is used, and it shows yet another definition of the word: "light upon" or "light on by chance." Jacob hadn't predetermined to spend the night there. He didn't choose the place in advance but was guided *by chance*—"because the sun was set."

Of course, we know the end of the story. The place, as it turns out, was a very special place—Bethel, which means "house of God." Jacob actually referred to it as a "gate of heaven." Even though most translations say Jacob lighted on "a" place, the literal Hebrew wording is "the" place. What was simply *a* place to Jacob, chosen by chance, was *the* place to the Lord and sovereignly chosen by Him. It was there that Jacob had a mighty, life-changing encounter with God. It was there that he saw the angels ascending and descending from heaven. It was at that time that God extended to him the same covenant He'd made with Abraham and informed Jacob that through his lineage He would save the world. He also promised great blessing to Jacob, to protect him and bring him back to his homeland safely. In short, it was a place where Jacob's entire destiny was foretold and his history shaped.

But remember, Jacob wasn't guided to this special place by his own reasoning or understanding. In the same way, we aren't always in a place to be directed in prayer either. Sometimes we may feel weak and ineffective in our ability to produce results in prayer. Often it can seem like a hit-or-miss process, as if we have to land or "light upon" the situation correctly "by chance."

That's OK. It's one of the primary meanings of *paga*.

The truth is, intercession is never a hit-or-miss deal, thanks to our Helper, the Holy Spirit. It's no coincidence that *paga* also means "bull's-eye."[1] In fact, they still use the word this way in Israel today. Close your eyes and fire! When we allow Him to intercede through us, He'll cause our prayers to light upon (*paga*) the right person or place, in the right way, at the right time, bringing about the will of God in situations. Who wouldn't want that kind of help in prayer?

Bethels will occur! Meetings with God will occur! Heaven's gates will open! Destinies will be written! History will be shaped!

Am I getting a little too melodramatic? Not on your life. Throughout time, God has proven that He *wants* to move through us. He *wants* miracles to happen, revival to break out, lives to be changed—and all through our prayers. One of the reasons we don't see more miracles is because we don't expect more miracles. Our Bible—on both sides of the Cross—presents a lot of them. They come from God, however, and the way to see more of them is to involve Him in more situations. Praying in the Spirit does this.

THE BUTTERFLY ANOINTING

Have you ever observed a butterfly flying from one location to another? It flutters this way and that, up and down, herky-jerky. It appears that it doesn't have the slightest idea where it's going. When I begin to pray in the Spirit, I sometimes feel like this. Whether I'm speaking in tongues, groaning or just uttering things I don't understand, I'll find my mind wandering this way

> "It's spiritual materialism when we evaluate our prayers by what we did while praying. 'Did I get excited, did I feel any strong emotions?' That's not the criteria at all. It's like Woody Allen said, 'Ninety percent of life is just showing up.' [With prayer] you show up, and you shut up. You can't do 'bad prayer'; you just cannot do it." —Brennan Manning[2]

and that, and I'll feel as though I'm trying to move in the "butterfly anointing."[3]

Where am I going? What am I doing? Will I land in the right place, on the right person? Is this really accomplishing anything?

But just as surely as that butterfly knows exactly where it's going, so the Holy Spirit directs my prayers precisely. They *will* "light upon" correctly.

I once heard a minister from Cleveland, Tennessee, tell a story that perfectly illustrates this. The guy was ministering in a small church in Canada for the first time and didn't know anyone in the church well. About 15 minutes into his message, he heard the Holy Spirit speak inwardly to him, *Stop your message and begin to pray in the Spirit.*

I'm sure you can imagine the awkwardness of such a thing, especially since he was with a group of strangers. But since he sensed the Holy Spirit's leading so strongly, he obeyed. "You'll have to excuse me," he said, "but the Lord has just instructed me to stop my message and pray in the Spirit." He began to pace the platform, praying in the Spirit audibly.

Five minutes went by. Nothing.

Ten minutes went by. Nothing.

Fifteen minutes went by. Still nothing.

I don't know about you, but I would've been feeling pretty nervous by that time. Talk about looking like you don't know what's going on. Talk about not knowing how to pray as he should—praying what was necessary, right or proper. Talk about needing to "light upon" by chance. Talk about the butterfly anointing!

Twenty minutes.

The people had simply sat and watched and listened as the man continued to pray in the Spirit. Suddenly a woman in the back began to scream, leaped to her feet and ran to the front of the church.

"What's happening?" the minister asked.

"My daughter is a missionary deep in Africa," the lady frantically began. "So deep, in fact, that it takes three weeks to get to where she is. You have to travel by automobile, then a boat, ride an animal and walk for a total of 21 days. My husband and I just yesterday received a telegram from the people she works with informing us that she had contracted a fatal disease that runs its course in three days. If she were in civilization, she could be treated; but it would take too long to get her there. 'She'll probably die within three days,' they told us, 'and all we can do is send you her body as soon as possible.'

"The last time my daughter was home," the lady continued, "she taught me some of the dialect of the people she works with. And I know this sounds crazy, but you just said, in that dialect, 'You can rejoice, your daughter is healed. You can rejoice, your daughter is healed.'"

And she was!

WOW! Now that's *PAGA*! That's lighting upon the right person at the right time in the right way. That's Holy Spirit help. That's the butterfly anointing.

Why did it take 20 minutes? Because it's a long way from Canada to Africa, and it took the Holy Spirit a while to flutter like a butterfly all that way?! Well, maybe not. I'm not sure why it took 20 minutes. There are several reasons why I believe perseverance is often necessary in prayer, but that's for another chapter. (Persevere and you'll get to it.)

"With" and Not "For"

Another tremendous way the Holy Spirit aids us in our intercession is hidden in the meaning of the word "helps." "And in the same way the Spirit also *helps* our weakness" (Rom. 8:26, emphasis added). The Greek word is *sunantilambanomai*. I think you have to speak in tongues just to say this word. There must be a revelation in it some-where. Actually, it's a compound word made up of three words. *Sun* means "together with," *anti* means "against," and *lambano* means "to take hold of."[4] Putting them together, a very literal meaning of the word would be "take hold of together with against."

How's that for help?

In situations when we're experiencing an inability to get results, the Holy Spirit not only wants to direct our prayers pre-cisely, causing them to light upon correctly, but He also wants to take hold of the situation together with us, adding His strength to ours. "'Not by [your] might not by [your] power, but by My Spirit,' says the Lord of hosts" (Zech. 4:6) will the mountain be moved.

Keep in mind one incredible element of this: The Holy Spirit doesn't just want to act *for* us; He wants to act *with* us. In other words, this isn't something He's simply doing in us—with or with-out our participation. We involve Him by praying in the Spirit, which is actually allowing Him to pray through us.

Several years ago, my wife, Ceci, developed a pain in her abdomen. What began as a minor discomfort grew in intensity over the course of a year, so she went to have it checked. The doc-tor found an ovarian cyst about the size of a large egg. He told us that surgery was necessary to remove it and possibly the ovary as well.

The doctor was a believer and understood spiritual principles, so I talked with him about giving us a little time to pray for heal-ing. "Doc," I said, "if you can give us some time, I think we can get rid of it by prayer."

"OK, I'll give you two months," he said, fairly confident that the cyst wasn't malignant or life threatening. "If you don't get it your way, we'll get it mine."

"Fair enough," I agreed.

We prayed for Ceci with every biblical method we knew of: laying on of hands; agreeing as a group; speaking the Scriptures;

elders anointing her with oil; binding, loosing, casting out, and, like good Charismatics, we even knocked her on the floor and let her lay there for a while. (Sometimes you just have to try everything!)

Through all this, nothing changed. I realized we were going to have to obtain this healing through perseverance and laying hold by faith (see 1 Tim. 6:12). That, by the way, is the way most answers to prayer come—not as instant miracles but through fighting the fight of faith and patience.

I felt that I needed to spend an hour a day praying for Ceci. I began my prayer times by stating my reason for approaching the Father. Then I referred to the Scriptures on which I was basing my petition. I would quote them, thanking the Father for His Word and thanking Jesus for providing healing. This usually took no more than five or six minutes. For the remainder of the hour I prayed in the Spirit. This went on for a month.

You might think that praying an hour a day for a month seems like a waste of time. God doesn't need that long to heal someone, right? I'm only telling you what worked for me. And I've discovered that the Lord doesn't have only one way of doing things, even the same things. His creative variety in working never seem to end. The key for us is always obedience.

So after a couple of weeks of praying each day specifically for my wife's healing, one afternoon the Lord showed me a picture as I was praying in the Spirit. I saw myself holding this cyst in my hand and squeezing the life out of it. I knew, of course, that I couldn't really get my hands on the cyst, but the Holy Spirit was showing me that as He prayed through me; *He* was "lighting on" and "taking hold with me against" the thing. Obviously, it was His power making the difference.

After seeing the picture of myself squeezing the life out of the cyst, I asked Ceci if there was any change in her condition. "Yes, the pain is decreasing," she informed me.

The doctor's response was, "If the pain is decreasing, the cyst must be shrinking. Keep doing whatever it is you're doing."

I tried hard to make sure I wasn't conjuring up any mental images, but twice more the Holy Spirit showed me this same picture. Each time the cyst was smaller. The last of them, which was the third time overall, was about a month into the process. In the picture, the cyst was about the size of a quarter. As I prayed, it vanished in my hand. I knew the Lord was letting me know the work was finished.

Three days later, Ceci informed me that all the pain and discomfort were gone. And the subsequent ultrasound confirmed what we already knew in our hearts—no more cyst!

You know what happened, don't you? *PAGA!*

- A "taking hold of together with against" happened.
- A "Bethel" happened.
- A "lighting on" happened.
- A "laying on" and "bearing away" happened.
- A "meeting" happened.
- An "enforcing" happened.
- A "representation" happened.

WEIGHTY INFLUENCE

A mouse and an elephant were best friends. They hung out together all the time, the mouse riding on the elephant's back. One day they crossed a wooden bridge, which began to bow, creak and sway under their weight. After they were across, the mouse, impressed over their ability to make such an impact, said to the elephant, "We sure shook up that bridge, didn't we?"

Intercession happened! And it can happen through you!

If you get nothing else from this book, remember this: God wants to use YOU. You don't have to be Mr. or Miss Wacko Charismatic Christian. You don't have to be the most well-known or popular believer in your youth group or at school. You don't have to know Greek from Swahili. All you have to be is a believer in Jesus. You're already one of His chosen representatives, one who is called and authorized to administer the blessings of the new covenant. Simply put, if you're a Christian, then you can be used.

God the Father wants to release the *work* of Jesus through your *prayers*. The Holy Spirit wants to help you. Bethels are waiting to be discovered. Histories are waiting to be written, destinies shaped.

Don't be intimidated by your age, your experience, or even your ignorance—not knowing what is "necessary, right or proper." Don't allow your weaknesses to paralyze you into inactivity. Rise up! Better still, allow your Helper to rise up in you! Together, you can shake any bridge!

Just make sure you understand who the mouse is.

PRAYER IN PRACTICE

*Holy Spirit, I know You're with me. Thank You for Your
awesome power. I pray that I'll rely on You more and more,
especially when I'm struggling for the right words, explanation
or answer for someone. Help my first priority to not be looking
good in front of others, but to genuinely lift them up in prayer
so that You can meet their needs. Teach me to hear Your voice
and sense Your movement more. I love You. Amen.*

THINGS THAT MAKE YA GO HMM...

1. When have you been frustrated in prayer by a lack of words or understanding? Does the Lord often burden you with a sense to pray yet with no reason why? Explain.
2. How does the Holy Spirit "help" us in our weaknesses?
3. In all honesty, are you willing to stick your neck on the line to wait on the Holy Spirit's guidance? In other words, would you risk appearing foolish for the sake of being obedient? If not (and you can be honest), what's holding you back?
4. After reading this chapter, what are some areas you feel led to offer up for the Holy Spirit's assistance?

Notes

1. Communicated to me by Israeli student Avi Mizrachi, at Christ for the Nations Institute in Dallas, Texas.
2. Michael Ciani, "An Afternoon with Brennan," *CCMMagazine.com*. http://ccm com.com/features/2278.aspx?Page=1 (accessed April 19, 2006).
3. The connection between Genesis 28:11-22 and Romans 8:26-28 along with several of the related thoughts, including the butterfly illustration, I first heard in a live message by Jack Hayford in Dallas, Texas, in 1976. He has since written about this in one of his books.
4. James Strong, *The New Strong's Exhaustive Concordance of the Bible* (Nashville, TN: Thomas Nelson Publishers, 1990), ref. no. 4878.

SUPERNATURAL CHILDBIRTH

CHAPTER 8

I was probably nine or ten years old the first time it happened to me.

I was lying in bed, thinking about my friends, recess, what I was going to do when school got out—you know, the typical things that keep a nine-year-old active boy from shutting his eyes. In the midst of my wide-eyed, wandering thoughts, I began to think about my aunt, who wasn't a Christian. I suddenly felt a burden to pray for her, so I muttered a few words. But as I did, the burden grew stronger and stronger. I remember getting out of my bed, onto my knees and weeping uncontrollably, asking God to save her. I was so young and it was so long ago that I can't remember how long it lasted—probably 30 minutes to an hour. Finally, the burden lifted and I went to sleep.

My aunt lived about an hour and a half away from us. For some "unknown" reason, she called us later that week and said she wanted to come to our church that Sunday morning. We didn't know at the time that she was actually coming to the service to give her life to Christ, and she did. I was amazed. I had travailed in prayer for her, and that very same week she drove the long distance to give her heart to the Lord. Talk about quick results!

I'd grown up in a church open to travailing in the spirit, and I'd seen it a few times, though it certainly sounded different from when I prayed for my aunt. But it was kind of a hush-hush deal— you know, one of those things too mysterious to be talked about. It was as if people wouldn't mention it for fear the "magic" might not come back. The truth was that this sort of intense and anguishing prayer just didn't seem to come upon anyone very often. And so it left me with a taboo question: If travailing intercession really helps get people saved, why wasn't it happening more often? Sure, it was loud and a bit weird, but who wouldn't want to be part of something that led to such immediate—and powerful—results?

THINGS AREN'T ALWAYS WHAT THEY APPEAR TO BE

Travailing—and other "strange" types of intercession—gets a bad rap. Apparently, it's controversial among Christians. So let me suggest a couple of things before we continue. First, I believe that biblical travail is an important, if not essential, part of intercession for the lost. Second, I don't believe it's defined by groaning, wailing, weeping and hard work. Natural travail—as when a woman gives birth to a child—certainly finds expression in these things; and spiritual travail *can* include these things. But I don't buy the argument that it *must* include them, and I'm convinced it's not defined by them. In fact, I believe that we can all travail while doing the dishes, mowing the lawn, driving a car—anything we can do and still pray.

Unfortunately, people have a need to see or feel something in order to believe in it (it's in our nature). Because of that, Christians tend to judge what's happening in the spirit by what we see naturally. For example, if we pray with someone for salvation or repentance, we tend to believe that the person who weeps is probably receiving more than the one who doesn't. We even say things such as, "The Holy Spirit really touched him or her," simply because we can see a reaction.

The truth is, I've seen some people who didn't cry or show any emotion while praying, and their lives were completely transformed. On the other hand, I've witnessed some who sobbed and wept in seeming repentance but experienced no change whatso-ever. It all boils down to this: *You can't judge what's happening in the realm of the spirit by what takes place in the natural realm.*

Some believers discount any "unexplainable" displays of the power of God. But it's important to realize that in any spiritual release of God's power and anointing, the possibility of a physi-cal manifestation always exists—that's biblical. People may weep. People may at times fall down under the power of God. People may laugh, perhaps hilariously. They may even appear drunk, just like those in the Early Church did. Sometimes when God moves, there is a physical manifestation; often there is not. But again, *you can never ever judge what's happening in the spirit by what you see in the natural.*

It's a Spiritual Thang

It's no different with travail. For some reason, the Holy Spirit chose to use a *physical* phenomenon—childbirth—to describe a *spiritual* happening or truth. The comparison isn't meant to be literal or exact. In other words, the Holy Spirit wasn't trying to describe what's happening *physically*, but rather what's happen-ing *spiritually*. It's not a natural birth; it's a spiritual one.

And that's what is meant to be emphasized—the *spiritual* power released to give birth *spiritually*, not the *physical* phenome-non that might accompany it. If you've ever been around people involved with travailing prayer, you know that what usually hap-pens is that the focus begins to turn toward the physical things— the groaning, weeping, wailing, crying out, etc. And as a result,

"Whenever we find the presence of the Holy Spirit, we will always find the supernatural." —Kathryn Kuhlman

you miss out on the spiritual point that something is being born in the Spirit.

Have you fallen into the same trap? It's easy to find out if you've made this mistake. Ask yourself this question and answer it honestly: When you hear the word "travail" in the context of prayer, is your first thought about *what* is taking place in the spirit (a birthing), or *how* it's happening outwardly (in the body)?

Most of us fall into the second category. We think of the manifestations. In fact, many of us get in the habit of defining a work of the Spirit by a work of the body. But when we make that our understanding of travail, we've not only missed the real issue, but we've also unconsciously accepted what I believe is a lie of Satan: that only a few people can really travail—and even then, only rarely.

The truth is, all of us can involve ourselves in travailing (birthing) intercession, and we can do it regularly. The key is to realize that the emphasis is on birthing something spiritually, not on what happens to us as we do it.

ARE YOU READY TO GIVE BIRTH?

Having said all that, let's get back to finding out what travailing—or what I like to call "birthing" prayer—*really* is. Did you know you were made to give birth? It doesn't matter if you're a guy or a girl—the Holy Spirit wants to "bring forth" things through you. Jesus said in John 7:38, "From his *innermost being* shall flow rivers of living water" (emphasis added). "Innermost being" is the word *koilia*, which means "womb."[1] As strange as it sounds, we are the womb of God upon the earth. We aren't the source of life, but we are *carriers* of the source of life. We don't generate life, but we release—through prayer—Him who does.

The key to doing this is the Holy Spirit. In fact, we don't birth anything spiritually; the Holy Spirit does. He's the birthing agent of the Godhead (see Luke 1:34-35; John 3:3-8). He's the power source of the Godhead (see Acts 1:8; 10:38; Luke 4:14,18), supplying motion to God's will and giving it life and substance. He's the power behind Creation which, as we'll see, is likened to a birthing (see Gen. 1). He gives birth to the will of God. He's the one who breathes God's life into people, bringing physical and spiritual life (see Gen. 2:7; Ezek. 37:9,10,14; Acts 2:1-4).

Got the point? We should never think we can take the credit for bringing anything about in the spirit—it's *always* the Holy Spirit who prompts change. Think about Elijah up on Mount Carmel (see 1 Kings 18:41-45). There was no way he could birth or produce rain. Yet James 5:17-18 tells us that his prayers did. Paul couldn't bring the Galatians to salvation, nor could he grow them up from being spiritual babies. Yet Galatians 4:19 implies that he experienced the pains of childbirth while praying for them, and the result was a flourishing Church. None of us can produce spiritual sons and daughters through our human abilities, yet Isaiah 66:7-8 tells us that our travail can. If we can't create or birth these and other things through our own power or ability, then it seems fairly obvious that our prayers must in some way cause or release the Holy Spirit to do so.

BROODING AND BIRTHING

Here's something cool: The Holy Spirit has been birthing things since before time began. The first words of the Bible read, "In the beginning . . . the earth was formless and void" (Gen. 1:1-2). Basically, the world as we know it was lifeless and sterile, with absolutely nothing going on. Verse 2 explains what changed the scene: "The Spirit of God was moving over the surface of the waters."

The Hebrew word used for "moving," *rachaph*, literally means "to brood over."[2] *The Amplified Bible* actually uses the words "was moving, hovering, brooding over." The margin of the *New American Standard Bible* also uses the word "hovering." So *rachaph* is a hovering or brooding over something.

What does it mean to brood? *Webster's Dictionary* defines "brood" as "offspring; progeny; that which is bred or produced."[3] A hen's brood, for example, is her chicks that she has produced. It comes from the root word "breed," which we know means giving birth to something.

In using this term to describe Creation, the Holy Spirit is using the analogy of "birthing" something. He was "bringing forth" life. Psalm 90:2 (*NIV*) confirms this, describing the Holy Spirit birthing the mountains and everything else. The verse uses two important Hebrew words, *yalad* [4] and *chuwl*.[5] It reads, "Before the mountains were born [*yalad*] or you brought forth [*chuwl*] the earth and the world, from everlasting to everlasting, you are God." These two Hebrew words, used throughout the Old Testament, both involve the same definitions: "to bring forth," "to be born," "to give birth to," "to travail."

JUST HOVERING AROUND

What does this have to do with prayer? Everything. These are the very same words used in Isaiah 66:8: "As soon as Zion *travailed* [*chuwl*] she also *brought forth* [*yalad*] her sons" (emphasis added). This is extremely important! *What the Holy Spirit was doing in Genesis when He "brought forth" or "gave birth to" the earth and the world is exactly what He wants to do through our prayers in bringing forth sons and daughters—the lost.* He wants to hover around individuals and release His awesome power to convict, break bondages, bring revelation and draw them to Himself in order to cause the new birth or new creation in them. Yes, *the Holy Spirit wants to birth through us.*

In fact, He has a reputation of birthing through whoever will let Him. Remember Abraham and Sarah? They were old—*really* old. Try 100 years old! There was absolutely no physical way they could have a baby. And yet when Moses recounts the couple's story as the parents of a nation, in Deuteronomy 32:10-18, he says that like an eagle hovers (*rachaphs*) over its young, the Lord hovered over them. The Holy Spirit brooded over Abraham and Sarah, releasing His life and power, giving them the ability to conceive and essentially birth an entire nation!

Or how about Mary, Jesus' mother? She found it hard to believe when an angel told her she would bear a child, since she was still a virgin. But the angel explained that the "Holy Spirit will come upon you, and the power of the Most High will over-shadow you" (Luke 1:35). "Overshadow" is the Greek word *episkiazo*, which means to cast a shade upon; to envelope in a haze of brilliancy; to invest with supernatural influence.[6]

It's the same word that's used in Acts 5:15 when people were trying to get close to Peter—in his shadow—so they could be healed. Have you ever wondered how Peter's shadow could heal anyone? It didn't. What was actually happening was that the Holy Spirit was "moving" out from Peter—hovering—and when individuals stepped into the cloud or overshadowing, they were healed.

Have you ever seen this phenomenon? I have. I've been in ser-vices where God was moving in such a strong way that before people were ever prayed for or touched by anyone, they were saved, healed or delivered. They came under the hovering of the Holy Spirit.

Maybe you've been in a meeting when the Spirit of the Lord began to hover over the whole room and move in a particular way. At times God has even done this over entire communities. If you've read about classic revivals of the past, you know that almost every revival has stories of people being compelled to walk into wherever the revival was taking place and ask to get saved. Countless individuals have traveled close to the place where God was moving in mighty ways and they began to weep, knowing that they needed to change their lives.

The point is that we can never forget who initiates, broods, hovers, births and changes lives. While the power-filled shadow is wonderful, the shadow-maker is even greater! If you're in a seemingly hopeless situation—one that appears to be as lifeless as a formless world or as hopeless as a 100-year-old woman's womb—consider your circumstances as ripe for the Holy Spirit's brooding. He's the one we need to be calling upon for change. Pray for His powerful hovering in whatever situation you're in.

ANYBODY GOT AN UMBRELLA?

Though it's the Holy Spirit who does the birthing and the changing, God invites *us* to be the ones through whom this change comes about. And that's where spiritual birthing comes in. When we experience spiritual travail, we release the creative power or

EVAN ROBERTS AND THE WELSH REVIVAL

Only 27 years old, Evan Roberts reluctantly became the face of the 1904-05 Welsh Revival. A quiet, reflective preacher who preferred talking with congregations rather than harsh Bible-thumping, Roberts led revival services by simply waiting on the Holy Spirit to move. Before revival began, his life had been changed by an experience in which he "was privileged to speak face-to-face with [God] as man speaks face-to-face with a friend" (see Exod. 33:11). The result of this and other prayer times? Almost 100,000 people came to Christ in a single year, and the daily life of an entire nation was drastically changed.

energy of the Holy Spirit into a situation to produce, create or give birth to something. Travailing intercession is simply the prayer that causes this.

Before wrapping up this chapter, I want to offer another area in which we can ask for the Holy Spirit's birthing: *revival*. Unfortunately, that word has become such an overused Christian term that many of us are tired of hearing about it. And, if I can be so blunt, I understand why—because we rarely, if ever, see *real* revival. It's more hype than reality. But here's the truth: Revival is what we—individuals, communities, cities, countries—desperately need. We need the rain of Holy Spirit-birthed revival to pour over us and cleanse every part of us.

That's why the story of Elijah that I mentioned earlier is so relevant to us today, especially as we talk about travailing intercession. In 1 Kings 18, Elijah prayed fervently seven times for rain. The passage even mentions that he prayed in the same position as a woman giving birth (v. 42). Why do you think God would make sure that detail was included? Don't you think He could've just told us that the prophet was praying for rain? Why such specific details as to *how* he was praying?

It's simple, really. Elijah's travail—his spiritual birthing—released physical rain. The message (not to mention the symbolism) is clear. Our travail releases the rain of the Spirit. It releases revival, salvation, healing, and more. Stuff really happens when we pray. Our prayers can and do cause the Holy Spirit to move into situations where He then releases His power to bring life. We do have a part in producing the hovering of the Holy Spirit.

But don't miss the important part of Elijah's story. *Even though it was God's will to bring the rain, and it was also God's time for the rain, someone on Earth still had to birth it through prayer.* What does this mean? It means the same thing we talked about earlier in this book: God needs you to re-present Him, to bring about the birthing of His will on Earth. Could He do it alone? Sure. But in His infinite wisdom, He has chosen to use you and me.

That kind of changes the perspective on travailing prayer, now doesn't it? Not only does this kind of intercession effect serious changes in the heavenlies, but it also brings new sons and daughters into the Kingdom! The same power that created the universe through His "*rachaph*-ing" has been deposited in every believer.

That's some serious *umph* behind a prayer!

PRAYER IN PRACTICE

Holy Spirit, I welcome Your hovering in my life. Brood over whatever things need to be rejuvenated, and birth what needs to be brought forth. Even though I sound like a skipping CD player, thank You once again for involving me in this process. I'm overwhelmed, and yet I want to be used by Your power. I lift up [names of unsaved friends and family] to You and ask You, Holy Spirit, to hover in their lives. Bring the rain of Your revival. Amen.

THINGS THAT MAKE YA GO HMM...

1. What kind of impression did you have of travailing prayer before this chapter? What experiences have you had dealing with this in the past?
2. In all honesty, do you often fall into the trap of "ranking" spiritual things according to physical manifestations? What are we supposed to do to avoid this?
3. What does it mean when people talk about the "moving" of the Holy Spirit?
4. How does Creation relate to our praying for the lost?

5. After reading this chapter, what are some areas over which you feel led to travail in prayer?

Notes

1. W. E. Vine, *The Expanded Vine's Expository Dictionary of New Testament Words* (Minneapolis, MN: Bethany House Publishers, 1984), p. 110.
2. William Wilson, *Old Testament Word Studies* (Grand Rapids, MI: Kregel Publications, 1978), p. 175.
3. *The Consolidated Webster Encyclopedic Dictionary* (Chicago, IL: Consolidated Book Publishers, 1954), p. 89.
4. James Strong, *The New Strong's Exhaustive Concordance of the Bible* (Nashville, TN: Thomas Nelson Publishers, 1990), ref. no. 3205.
5. Ibid., ref. no. 2342.
6. Ibid., ref. no. 1982.

HOW TO BECOME A PRO WRESTLER

CHAPTER 9

Resist the devil and he will flee from you! How many of you talk to the kingdom of darkness once in a while?" I asked in my most anointed preaching voice.

I was on a roll—preaching up a storm, as we said back in Ohio where I was raised. I was fresh out of Bible school and feeling like the next Billy Graham. I had those people right where I wanted them, hanging on every word. The only problem was that I was in Guatemala preaching through an interpreter.

Why was that a problem? you ask.

Because my interpreter didn't seem to share my theology, and her convictions ran deep. She looked at me indignantly and said in no uncertain terms, "I won't say that!"

Her words kind of interrupted my eloquent flow. "Huh?" I replied.

"I won't say that."

"What do you mean you won't say it? You're supposed to say what I say."

"Well, I won't say it."

"Why not?"

"I don't believe in it."

"Well, the Bible says to do it."

"Where?"

"James 4:7."

Now, keep in mind that we were standing in front of a church full of people who were watching this obviously unpleasant verbal exchange between Mr. Foreign Preacher-man and his interpreter.

I hadn't been prepared for this in Bible school. As I stood wondering what to do next, my interpreter began to look for James 4:7. Took her forever to find it. She then read it to the audience (I think). For all I know, she could've been telling them how stupid I was.

We tried to continue. But she wouldn't allow me to quote any other verses. As I'd mention one, she'd take her time finding it and would read it aloud (I think). Didn't take me long to figure out she didn't know her Bible very well, so I started paraphrasing verses so she wouldn't recognize them as Scripture. After she had unknowingly said the verse, I'd look at her with a smug smile and say, "That was found in . . ." She didn't appreciate that and often returned my comment with a glare from her very unspiritual eyes.

We never did seem to get that flow back.

WHICH SIDE ARE YOU ON?

Intercession, according to our definition, involves two very different activities. One is a *reconciling*; the other is a *separating*. One is a *tearing away*—a disuniting; the other is a *joining to*—a uniting. This is what Christ did through His work of intercession, and it's what we do in our continuation of His work. In light of this, it's important to realize that much of our intercession must be a combination of both.

Unfortunately, most Christians tend to embrace one part of intercession or the other—to the extreme. Many, like my interpreter in Guatemala, refuse to believe in spiritual warfare. They suppose that since Jesus took care of the devil at Calvary, we don't need to concern ourselves with him. Then there's the other side—the ones who get all the bad press.

I remember seeing a cartoon that portrayed the devil with 40 to 50 strands of rope around him and several individuals next to him discussing the situation.

"What do we do now?" one asked.

"I say we bind him again!" was the response of another.

Which extreme do you relate to? I hope that since you're reading this book, you're willing to embrace both.

CAN'T TAKE THE PRAYER OUT OF WARFARE

As we discovered earlier, it's impossible to separate the word "intercession," *paga*, from warfare. Like it or not, violence and war are rooted in the very meaning of the word. When we try to separate warfare from intercession, we lose out. A lot of times we waste time and energy dealing with symptoms when the real cause of the problem is spiritual or demonic: "For we wrestle not against flesh and blood, but against principalities, against powers, against the rulers of the darkness of this world, against spiritual wickedness in high places" (Eph. 6:12, *KJV*). Obviously, we need to guard against overemphasizing Satan and his demons. But we in America tend to err in the other direction. Most people stop in Ephesians 6:12 after the words, "we wrestle not."

Our ignorance of the enemy's tactics—as well as how to deal with them—is costly for us. Second Corinthians 2:11 tells us: "In order that no advantage be taken of us by Satan; for we are not ignorant of his schemes." Though this verse is talking about forgiveness, the general principle is clear: When we're unaware of the enemy's schemes, he takes advantage of us.

I once heard about a teenager who could never achieve any stability in life or in his walk with the Lord. He would excel at school, and then fall in with the wrong crowd and end up in trouble; he would walk with the Lord for a while, and then turn

"The devil is aware that one hour of close fellowship, hearty converse with God in prayer, is able to pull down what he hath been contriving and building many a year."
—John Flavel

away again. This cycle repeated itself again and again with no amount of prayer seeming to make a difference.

One day as a minister was praying for this young man, the Lord showed him a picture of three demons that were following the fellow everywhere he went. They were not in him, but they were always there to influence him. The minister saw names over each demon, describing what they did. One at a time he bound them in Jesus' name and commanded them to leave the youth alone.

From that moment on, everything changed. Stability came. Success followed. Eventually the teenager grew up to become a wealthy businessman as well as a minister. And he's still walking with God today. It's always good and right to ask the Father to strengthen and mature individuals, but this guy needed something more, someone to exercise authority and enact a deliverance. His instability was the symptom of demonic influence that he couldn't overcome by himself. Satan had the advantage, and as long as his schemes remained hidden, he prevailed.

Maybe you're still a little uncertain about this whole spiritual warfare thing. I'll admit, it's a tricky area that a lot of Christians get hung up on. But the good thing is, we can look to the Bible for proof that not only does it exist, but also that God calls us to it. Here are a few definites we know about warring in the spirit.

- We are in a very real war (see 2 Cor. 10:4; 1 Tim. 1:18).
- We are soldiers in this war (see Ps. 110:2-3; 2 Tim. 2:3-4).
- We are to wrestle against all levels of the kingdom of darkness (see Eph. 6:12).
- We are to resist the devil (which would in most situations be his demons) and he will flee from us (see Jas. 4:7; 1 Pet. 5:9).
- We are to tread on Satan and his demons (i.e., exercise authority over them; see Luke 10:19; Rom. 16:20).
- We are to cast out demons (see Mark 16:17).

- We have authority to bind (forbid) and loose (permit) when dealing with the agents and gates of hell (see Matt. 16:19).
- We have powerful weapons designed to overcome the kingdom of darkness (see 2 Cor. 10:4; Eph. 6:10-20).

This certainly isn't an exhaustive list of warfare Scriptures, but it simply shows that God takes it seriously—and so should we.

IT'S SMACK-DOWN TIME!

In spiritual warfare, the point isn't so much how we wrestle but that we do wrestle. Notice that none of the Scripture references listed above are defensive in nature. They're all offensive. We are to aggressively deal with and come *against* the forces of darkness whenever the challenge or opportunity arises.

That word "against" is used five times in Ephesians 6. The word in Greek is *pros*, which is a strengthened form of *pro*. *Pro* means "in front of,"[1] either literally or figuratively (in the sense of superior to). We use the concept today in the word "professional," or in its shortened form "pro." A pro athlete is one who is "in front of" or "superior to" others. *Pros* also has the connotation of stepping forward and facing toward something or someone.[2] The symbolism in this Ephesians passage is of a wrestler stepping forward and facing his opponent. Basically, God is saying to us, "Step forward and face the powers of darkness. Be a pro wrestler!"

Don't be like the bodybuilder who was visiting Africa and was asked by a village chief what he did with all his muscles. The bodybuilder thought an exhibition might better serve to explain it, so he proceeded to flex his bulging calves, thighs, biceps and triceps, demonstrating how he performed in competition. After admiring this amazing specimen for a few moments, the chief inquired, "What else do you use them for?"

"That's about it," answered the muscular man.

"That's all you use those huge muscles for?" reiterated the chief.

"Yes."

"What a waste," muttered the chief in disgust. "What a waste."

A lot of us are like this bodybuilder. We're strong in the Lord, well-equipped to deal with our adversary, but we never use our strength or our weapons. Step into the ring! As we wait upon the Lord, He'll show us which strategy or method of warfare to use.

GOD'S TIMING, GOD'S TERMS, GOD'S METHOD

The problem is, a lot of us march into combat without getting our marching orders from the Commander-in-Chief. The results are usually disastrous. Instead, we need to spend quality intimate time worshiping and waiting on God. That keeps us from becoming reactionary to the devil. Remember, our response isn't to the devil. We do nothing on his terms, nor are we to do anything in his timing. God chooses the times of battle. He told Joshua at Jericho (see Josh. 6), as he was on his face in worship, "Seven days, Joshua. Not a moment before. Don't do anything until I tell you." He was saying, "I choose the timing of battle."

God also chose the terms. "Take no prisoners—only Rahab escapes. The spoils are to be given to Me. I choose the terms—you don't, Satan doesn't, no one else does. If you do it My way, you'll always win. Do it the devil's way and you'll find yourself walking in circles." God chose the timing, the terms and the method. Warfare isn't responsive reaction but responsible action. It must be born from obedience, not necessity. We follow our Captain, not our foe.

At times, God may say that worship is the key, as it was for Jehoshaphat on the battlefield (see 2 Chron. 20:1-30) and for Paul and Silas in the jail (see Acts 16:16-36). Years ago I had the chance to minister with 200 other believers on the streets of New Orleans during Mardi Gras. On one occasion, the Lord led us to march silently down the streets. An awesome fear of the Lord and

A MATTER OF AUTHORITY

A lot of people wonder why spiritual warfare is needed in the first place if Jesus already defeated Satan and his demons. Didn't He already deliver us from Satan's power?

The answer lies in understanding what Christ actually did when He defeated Satan. Satan's destruction wasn't a literal one, but rather a legal breaking of his headship or authority. Nowhere does the Bible say Christ delivered us from Satan's power. It says He delivered us from his *exousia*—authority; or in other words, the right to use his power on us (check out Col. 1:13 and Luke 10:19 for more on this).

Power never was and never will be the issue between God and Satan. Authority was the issue—the authority Satan had obtained back when Adam messed up. Jesus didn't come to get back any power or to remove Satan's power. He came to regain the authority Adam lost to the serpent and break Satan's headship over the earth.

Satan still has all the inherent powers and abilities he has always had. He "prowls about like a roaring lion" (1 Pet. 5:8)—and he's still got some mean teeth. He still has "fiery darts" (Eph. 6:16, *KJV*). So when we engage in spiritual warfare, we're not doing the fighting, nor are we mustering up any power to defeat Satan again. We're simply reminding him who we belong to, who has already claimed us for life and who has all authority. Say the name "Jesus"? Yeah, there's no doubt he'll remember the One who kicked his tail ages ago.

the presence of God began to hover over the entire area. The Lord had established His awesome presence and silenced His foes. A literal hush came to the streets.

On another occasion, however, He led us to march down the middle of Bourbon Street, praising and worshiping out loud. This time a spirit of conviction began to hover over the street as we sang a powerful song that spoke of humanity's true destiny. As before, a silence came. It seemed as though the Lord had totally taken charge. At one intersection, which was blocked off for foot traffic, we gathered in a circle on our knees and continued to sing. As we knelt worshiping, a man literally ran into our circle, crying out that he wanted to know God.

That's praise warfare! It's also intercession (*paga*)—attacking the enemy. As Christ is enthroned in worship, Satan is dethroned in the heavenlies (see Pss. 22:3; 149:5-9). As we lift up the Son, we pull down the serpent.

Other times, the Holy Spirit's strategy might include acts of kindness, giving, forgiving or simply hanging out with a rough crowd. In essence, we defeat the darkness through the simplicity of Christlike love. Warfare through humility. Violent love. Seems pretty paradoxical, doesn't it?

CAN I GET A SHOUT OUT?

As you can see, there are certain times when aggressive, violent spiritual warfare in intercession is needed. Sometimes it even includes something that may be a little outside your comfort zone: shouting. Though this isn't about reaching a certain volume to rebuke evil forces, the Bible is specific that at times, raising our voices to whatever's opposing us is exactly what drives it home.

- Zerubbabel shouted grace to a mountain (see Zech. 4:7).
- Israel shouted at Jericho (see Josh. 6:16).

- Gideon's army shouted before the battle (see Judg. 7:20).
- Jesus shouted on the cross (see Matt. 27:50).
- Israel shouted when the Ark of the Covenant would lead them to a new place (see Num. 10:35; Ps. 68:1).

I'm not trying to start the First Church of the Screaming Warriors, but I am trying to show that warfare, even intense and sometimes loud warfare, is valid. Let's not be like Joash, the king of Israel who was rebuked and suffered defeat because he lacked spiritual intensity in striking with the arrows (see 2 Kings 13:14-19).

At other times, the strategy of the Lord may be to simply speak the Word as a sword or make biblically based declarations into the situation. When led by the Holy Spirit, this strategy is devastating to the enemy.

On one occasion, I was trying to mediate a peace between three parties. It had gotten so bad that one guy even told me that the following morning he was going to get physical. I knew he meant it and that someone would be hurt and others would be in jail. So I stayed up late praying, pleading with God to stop this when, at around 2:00 A.M., the Lord shocked me with these words: *Why are you begging Me to do this? You know My will in this situation. And the problem is being caused by a spirit of anger and violence. Bind it! Declare My Word and will into the situation.*

I did and went to bed. The next morning, for some "unexplainable" reason, without any discussion, everyone had a change of heart. Peace and harmony ruled where the night before violence and anger had reigned. What had happened?

Paga happened.

Calvary happened.

Psalm 110:2 happened: "The LORD will stretch forth Your strong scepter from Zion, saying, 'Rule in the midst of Your enemies.'"

IT'S FOR REAL, DUDE

The purpose of this chapter isn't to psych you up to go head to head with Satan and all his darkness. As I said earlier, we've got to remember that God is the one who's already done the fighting. Our part is to *re*-present His authority in the earth, to remind our opponent (who never seems to get the clue that he's already lost) of the final outcome, thanks to Jesus' work on the cross.

However, as long as we're breathing, there will be a battle raging in the spirit. And our part in intercession is simply to aggressively come against the enemy and thwart his efforts. Warfare is for real and is a crucial part of intercession. Sometimes, we'll even be prompted to do some pretty radical things to declare God's victory. But you can't deal with intercession—*paga*—without mentioning warfare. We must engage in it with balance and understanding, but *we must do it!* To ignore Satan is to abdicate to Satan.

In the next chapter, we'll apply this concept of warfare to praying for the lost. We have a vital role to play in setting the captives free. Let's make a gain on the kingdom of darkness!

PRAYER IN PRACTICE

Father, once again I'm blown away by the fact that
You choose to use me in matters of the Spirit. I praise You
not only because You've already won the ultimate victory,
but that You lead me into a war where You do all the
fighting. Holy Spirit, I pray that You'll remove any
blinders that Satan has put on me that keep me from
recognizing his schemes. Help me know Your timing
and Your methods of how to engage in battle through
my prayers. Lead me to victory. Amen.

THINGS THAT MAKE YA GO HMM...

1. What are the two opposite activities usually needed in intercession? Why are both necessary?
2. How has Satan pulled the wool over our eyes? In what ways has he blinded believers when it comes to spiritual warfare?
3. How does spiritual warfare involve waiting?
4. Why do we have to do spiritual warfare at all? Didn't Jesus already win the battle?

Notes

1. Geoffrey W. Bromiley, *Theological Dictionary of the New Testament Abridged* (Grand Rapids, MI: William B. Eerdmans Publishing Co., 1985), p. 935.
2. James Strong, *The New Strong's Exhaustive Concordance of the Bible* (Nashville, TN: Thomas Nelson Publishers, 1990), ref. no. 4314.

WAR TACTICS

CHAPTER 10

I was never great at math when I was in school. It was as if there was a fog around my brain anytime someone would try to explain a new algorithm or formula to me. I knew what the purpose was, and I could grasp what was going on with certain numbers and variables, but without fail, *something* wouldn't click. Sure, I could see what was going on—I just couldn't fully understand it.

The Bible says that it's the same way when unbelievers try to grasp the gospel. In fact, 2 Corinthians 4:3-4 calls it a "veil," which means "to hide, cover up, wrap around," just like the inside of a tree is veiled by bark or the inside of a human body is veiled by skin.[1] The Greek word is *kalupsis*, and if you add the prefix *apo* to make *apokalusis*, you get the New Testament word for "revelation." *Apo* means "off or away,"[2] so literally, a revelation is an unveiling, an uncovering.

This chapter is all about spiritual warfare for the lost. It may be the most important chapter in this book because it deals with how you and I can influence the eternal destinies of other people. We have a part to play in lifting the veil off the mind of the unbeliever. The passage above tells us there is a veil or covering over the minds of unbelievers that keeps them from clearly seeing the light of the gospel. It's important to know that *they don't see the gospel because they can't see it. They don't under-*

> "And even if our gospel is veiled, it is veiled to those who are perishing, in whose case the god of this world has blinded the minds of the unbelieving, that they might not see the light of the gospel of the glory of Christ, who is the image of God." —2 Corinthians 4:3-4

stand it because they can't understand it. They must have an unveiling—a revelation.

WHAT-EVER

We live in a time in which everything is relative. *Whatever works for you, man.* That seems to be our society's motto not only for how we live but also for what we believe. It's the reason why you can preach the gospel message to someone until you're blue in the face, and the only response you'll get is a sincere, "I'm glad that's made a difference for you. But for me, well, I kinda like how my life's going." A friend of mine from Alaska told me about a guy he was witnessing to who just wasn't getting it. "I know there's something to what you're saying," the guy said to my friend, "because it's obvious what it's done for you. But I can't yet fully *see it.*"

I used to struggle with how in the world some people could hear amazing stories and presentations of the gospel yet flat-out reject it. Now I know. When "hearing" it, they weren't hearing what I heard, they weren't seeing what I saw, or understanding what I understood. What they heard was filtered through a belief system—a veil—that caused them to hear something totally different.

It's like the story of a woman who was driving home alone one evening when she noticed a man in a large truck following her. She got scared and sped up, trying to lose her pursuer, but it was futile. She then exited the freeway and drove up a main street, but the truck stayed with her, even running red lights to do so.

In a panic, the woman wheeled into a service station, jumped from her car and ran inside screaming. The truck driver ran to her car, jerked the back door open and pulled from the floor behind her seat a man who was hiding there.[3]

The lady was fleeing from the wrong person. *She was running from her savior!* The truck driver, perched high enough to see into her back seat, had spied the would-be rapist and was pursuing her to save her, even at his own risk.

Just like this lady's, the perspective of unbelievers is distorted. People run from the pursuit of a God who desires to save them from destruction. Maybe it's because they've had a bad experience with hypocritical Christians in the past, or because they've been abused and felt like God never came through for them. The truth of who He is, however, remains veiled.

INFORMATION VS. REVELATION

Unfortunately, a lot of people think they've "tried God" simply because they went to church a couple times, learned about Him when they were young or read a few pages from the Bible. In their minds, "getting" God is just like "getting" a math equation. But when it comes to experiencing God, there's a huge difference between *information* and *revelation*. Information is of the mind; biblical revelation, however, involves and affects the mind but originates from the heart. Information can come immediately, but revelation is normally a process—and a life-changing one at that.

"He's more on the straight and narrow with his Christian views and I can respect that. I definitely don't agree with it, but if that's working for him . . . I don't want to judge anybody because of what they do."
—Korn singer Jonathan Davis, giving a relativistic take on former bandmate and guitarist Brian "Head" Welsh's decision to accept Christ into his life[4]

Jesus told a parable about the sower and the seeds. In short, it demonstrates that all biblical truth comes in seed form. Early in my walk with the Lord, I was frustrated because the wonderful truths I'd heard from some outstanding teachers weren't working for me. Sure, I had heard the teachings and they had really affected me. I remember leaving the meetings saying to myself, *I will never be the same!* And yet a few weeks or months later, I was the same.

As I complained to God and questioned the truth of what I'd heard, the Lord spoke words to me that have radically changed my life: *Son, all truth comes to you in seed form. It may be fruit in the person sharing it, but it is seed to you. Whether or not it bears fruit depends on what you do with it.* Spiritual information seeds must grow into fruit-producing revelation.

Knowledge or information alone—which is what humans have glorified and where they have begun their quest for meaning ever since the Fall—doesn't produce salvation. It doesn't necessarily lead to a true knowledge of God. Jesus said to the Pharisees, "You search the Scriptures, because you think that in them you have eternal life; and it is these that bear witness of Me" (John 5:39).

The Pharisees knew the Scriptures backward and forward, but they didn't know God. Many theologians today know the Scriptures thoroughly but don't know God well. Some, perhaps, don't know Him at all. They couldn't sit quietly in His presence for two hours without being bored to tears. They have much information, but little or no revelation. Revelation makes the Scriptures "spirit and life" (John 6:63). It makes them live.

Why is this so important? Because it's revelation that leads to biblical faith and true change. There are a million self-help books out there that may motivate you to try harder, live better, do good things—but none of them can help save your soul. None of them will bring about that "A-ha!" moment in which the light goes on to illuminate our ultimate need for salvation. Without this revelation, we're simply appealing to a fallen, selfish, humanistic mind that always asks, "What's in it for me? How can I better myself?"

Doesn't it make sense, then, why the gospel sounds so funky in contrast to this? In fact, our gospel is often ridiculous or moronic to nonbelievers: "But a natural man does not accept the things of the Spirit of God; for they are foolishness to him, and he cannot understand them, because they are spiritually appraised" (1 Cor. 2:14). The word "foolishness" is *moria*, from which we get the word "moron." Think about it: Who in his or her right mind *wants* to give up everything for the sake of Christ? Who *wants* to lay down his or her life—even unto death—for the good news of Jesus?

I'll tell you who: Those who have had the veil removed. Only when that happens can we see how truly pitiful we are by nature. Only when the Spirit of God reveals our true state can we acknowledge that we need a Savior.

RAISING THE WHITE FLAG

So what are we supposed to do if the only way people can accept the gospel is by the Spirit removing the veil from their eyes? We pray. I know what you're thinking: *Duh—isn't that the point of this book?* OK, more specifically, we pray for the Holy Spirit to birth true repentance in them through God-given revelation. Why repentance? Because from repentance comes the lowering of emotional walls, the softening of a hardened heart and the opening of eyes that were sealed shut by pride. Repentance is basically the white flag thrown up, saying, "OK, I give up. I can't do this anymore!"

A few years ago, a lady I'll call Sarah told me about how she had prayed for her sister and brother-in-law. Although generally nice people, she said that "they were very anti-Christian and were my husband's and my greatest persecutors spiritually, mocking and making fun of us."

Sarah had been praying for them *for 20 years*, but they'd shown no interest in the gospel. "Because of their attitude toward God and the gospel," Sarah admits, "I had developed a hard heart toward them. I was religiously proud against them and praying out of a wrong motive."

After listening to me teach on intercession, Sarah's hope was renewed and the Holy Spirit prompted her with the question, *When are you going to do this for your family?* She repented of her attitude, got her heart right and forgave them for their attitude toward God. Then she began to pray as I'd instructed.

Sarah's need to repent and change her own attitude is a valuable lesson for us. Our attitudes often keep God from being able to answer our prayers. Isn't it ironic and tragic that our own sin might hinder our prayers for another sinner? Jesus said, "First take the log out of your own eye, and then you will see clearly to take the speck out of your brother's eye" (Matt. 7:5). You may need to forgive your friend or classmate before God can use you to deliver him or her.

Sarah prayed several things, but among them she remembers specifically asking for "the veil to be lifted off of their eyes so they can see and understand the truth of the gospel." Along with that, she prayed "that they would come to Christ together so one would not persecute the other."

A couple of months later—remember, before applying these principles and dealing with her own heart Sarah had prayed for *20 years*—she called to speak with her sister. She heard this amazing report: Earlier that day her brother-in-law woke up with a strange feeling that he and his wife needed to go to church. (They *never* went to church.) So they found a small church, and during the altar call *both of them gave their lives to Christ*. Sarah's sister then apologized to Sarah for the way they had treated her. Their attitudes were completely changed. About nine months later, Sarah's father also came to the Lord.

Amazing, huh? This will work for you, too!

YES, YOU GET TO BLOW UP STUFF!

Now, wait. Before you say, "Yeah, right" and list all the reasons why the person you're praying for is virtually prayer-proof, let's look at some of the things—strongholds—that keep an unbeliever from seeing the truth. Maybe you've heard people at church toss around the word "stronghold" before but never quite understood what it meant. (We believers have a bad habit of talking in Christianese, don't we?) Actually, "stronghold" isn't necessarily a Christian term; it's often used in war. It's literally a place from which to *hold* something *strongly*—for example a fort, a castle or a prison. I've seen pictures of foxholes and trenches hastily dug in times of war to maintain a position. That's a hold. On the other hand, I toured a huge castle on top of a mountain in Salzburg, Austria, several years ago. From this seemingly impregnable fortress on a hill, someone had ruled the territory. That's a stronghold!

Satan has a place of strength *within* unbelievers from which he can hold on to them strongly. They are prisoners, captives, slaves. Yet Christ was sent "to proclaim release to the captives" (Luke 4:18). And as we re-present the victory of Jesus to the forces of darkness through warfare intercession, we can hone in on some specific spiritual strongholds. In fact, 2 Corinthians 10:3-5 reads like a "How to" guide for bringing down these fortified areas as we fight for the lost:

> For though we walk in the flesh, we do not war according to the flesh, for the weapons of our warfare are not of the

flesh, but divinely powerful for the destruction of fortresses. We are destroying speculations and every lofty thing raised up against the knowledge of God, and we are taking every thought captive to the obedience of Christ.

Mind-sets

The first aspect of the stronghold mentioned here is "speculations"—*logismos*. It's the Greek word from which we get the word "logic." A person's logic is the entire system of reasoning and rationale behind everything he or she thinks and believes. It includes philosophies, religions, humanism, atheism, past experiences, racism, materialism, roots of rejection, perversions—anything that causes a person to think a certain way and therefore creates a mind-set.

So how do these *logismos* blind individuals? How do they veil truth? By filtering *every single* notion through an already established system of beliefs. When unbelievers listen to the gospel message, they don't just hear the gospel; they also hear the resounding echoes of what they already believe.

For example, I was sharing the gospel with a teenage girl who'd been horribly abused. "God is love," I said. "He loves you so much that He sent His Son to die for you."

She heard me. But louder than my voice were the internal screams of past hurts, which came railing out against me. "Oh, really? If He's love, then why'd He allow me to get hurt so badly? Doesn't sound like a loving God to me."

That's a *logismos*—her beliefs, philosophies, wisdom, logic. It's also a powerful stronghold filled with rationale and hardened opinions. So how does the gospel break through these arguments? With persistent, targeted prayer that plows the ground before words are ever exchanged.

Perhaps you already know what these *logismos* are in the person for whom you're praying. If not, ask the Holy Spirit to reveal them to you. He will. And when He does, call them by name, quoting 2 Corinthians 10:3-5. Say, "In the name of the Lord Jesus Christ, I am destroying you, stronghold of . . ." Do it daily until the person comes to Christ.

Pride

The second part of the stronghold we must demolish is "every *lofty thing* raised up against the knowledge of God." This is referring to the same root of pride that came to humanity at the Fall when Adam and Eve bought the lie, "You too shall be as God" (see Gen. 3:5). It's the ultimate pride that characterizes being high-minded and inflated with self-conceit. (Fascinatingly enough, the words "pride" and "blindness" share the same original root word, *tupho*, which means "to make smoke." Indeed, pride itself creates a layer of smog so thick that you can't see out—which is exactly how Satan wants it to be!)

In our natural state, which is one of pride, we exalt ourselves against the knowledge of God. And that's why the unbeliever is trapped in a fog of refusing to believe the gospel. The good news is that we can tear down this stronghold in people through spiritual warfare so that they can humble themselves and bow their knees to Christ. Read 2 Corinthians 10:5 again in *The Living Bible*:

> These weapons *can* break down *every* proud argument against God and *every* wall that can be built to keep men from finding Him. With these weapons I *can* capture rebels and bring them back to God, and change them into men whose hearts' desire is obedience to Christ (emphasis added).

I like the "cans" and "everys" in the verse. The Lord doesn't wish us luck or tell us that we'll win a few once in a while. He lets us know that we *can* break down *every* proud argument and *every* wall; we *can* capture rebels! And we must!

Thoughts and Temptations

The Lord also tells us that we can "take every thought captive to the obedience of Christ." The word "thought" is *noema*, which also means plans, schemes, devices or plots. It refers to the spontaneous thoughts and temptations that Satan uses to assault the unbelievers, as well as the schemes and plans he uses to keep them in darkness. Have you ever been having a perfectly good day when all of sudden your mind is filled with a sexually explicit image or a string of curse words? It may be an inappropriate scene you saw in a movie years ago, yet Satan will use it against you in an attempt to trip you up.

Now imagine the power he has over your non-Christian friend's mind, which has yet to be yielded to the mind of Christ. It's hard enough to refrain from this stuff when your hormones go nuts during the teenage years, much less with Satan piling up the attack. And that's exactly why it's so important that in intercession we boldly declare that no weapon of Satan's will prosper. We must bind his plans and stand against them through prayer. We can and should pray that the unbeliever be shielded from Satan's thoughts and temptations.

GOD'S HOLY DETONATORS

As there always is with God, there's good news: We have weapons that are "divinely powerful" to pull down strongholds. The problem is that most of us don't even realize it. The word "powerful" is *dunatos*[5] and is actually one of the New Testament words for a miracle. Empowered by God, these weapons will work miracles. Empowered by our own efforts, they'll be complete duds. Let's not forget that *He's* the one who does the fighting, not us.

The word "powerful" is also translated "possible." I like that. Do you have a friend who seems impossible? Will it take a miracle to break through his walls of unbelief? With this power, he can become possible. And, of course, this is the Greek word from which we get the word "dynamite." This stuff is explosive!

This dynamite is explosive for the "destruction of fortresses" or, as the *King James Version* says, is capable of "pulling down strongholds." "Destruction" and "pull down" are the word *kathairesis*. This important and powerful word has a couple of pertinent meanings. One of them is "to bring down with violence or demolish" something.[6] With this powerful, miracle-working dynamite behind our weapons, we can become demolition agents violently tearing down Satan's strongholds.

Have you ever witnessed a demolition? As a small child, I watched the destruction of an old brick school. I was fascinated as the huge cement ball attached to a gigantic crane swung into the building time after time, crashing through walls and ceilings, bringing incredible destruction. I suppose this would be, in one sense, a practical picture of our warfare as we systematically—one divine blow at a time—work destruction on the strongholds of darkness. In fact, it usually happens this way—a systematic, ongoing, one-blow-at-a-time war against Satan's stronghold.

Then a few years ago I watched a huge building in Dallas, Texas, get demolished. Unlike the one I saw as a kid, this structure covered nearly an entire city block. The demolition crew didn't use a wrecking ball for this one. And it didn't take days. They used dynamite strategically placed by experts to demolish this massive building in less than 10 seconds.

This is also a picture of our intercession. Unlike this physical building, we don't usually see the answer in seconds—we may be strategically placing the dynamite of the Spirit for days, weeks or months. But every time we take up our spiritual weapons and use them against the strongholds of the enemy, we are placing our explosive charges in strategic places. And sooner or later the Holy Detonator of Heaven is going to say, "Enough!" There will be a mighty explosion in the spirit, a stronghold will crumble to the ground and a person will fall to his or her knees.

Now that's some serious power!

PRAYER IN PRACTICE

Father, Your power is awesome. I'm amazed by the fact that, like a giant sports stadium getting demolished, you can tear down the strongholds in an unbeliever through my prayers. Lead me as I confront the tactics of Satan and, by Your Spirit, take the veil off of people's eyes. Thank You for Your incredible victory! Amen.

THINGS THAT MAKE YA GO HMM...

1. How are people veiled from the truth?
2. How is it that someone can have all the Bible knowledge in the world yet not know God?
3. What is a stronghold? What are three specific strongholds that Satan uses to keep a grip on unbelievers?
4. How can you pray specifically against each of these strongholds?
5. Why can we be sure that our prayers are really doing something to blow up these strongholds?

Notes
1. Spiros Zodhiates, *The Complete Word Study Dictionary* (Iowa Falls, IA: Word Bible Publishers, 1992), p. 816.

2. James Strong, *The New Strong's Exhaustive Concordance of the Bible* (Nashville, TN: Thomas Nelson Publishers, 1990), ref. no. 575.

3. Craig Brian Larson, *Illustrations for Preaching and Teaching* (Grand Rapids, MI: Baker Books, 1993), p. 98.

4. "Korn on Head." http://www.mtv.com (accessed October 10, 2005).

5. Strong, *The New Strong's Exhaustive Concordance,* ref. no. 1415.

6. Ibid., ref. no. 2507.

THE LIGHTNING OF GOD

CHAPTER 11

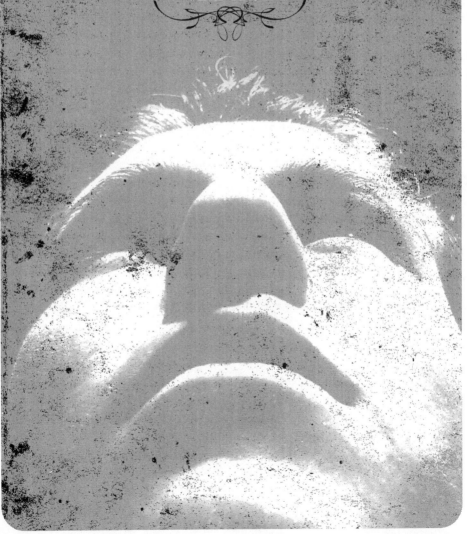

This was just about the coolest thing I'd discovered since baseball. I was in the fifth grade, in that ornery but not mean, "can't stand baths," "all girls have cooties" stage of life. And I had recently gotten my first magnifying glass.

I'm not sure how I discovered that I could hold a magnifying glass at just the right angle to the sun and catch a piece of paper on fire. I didn't do anything majorly bad, like the time I nearly burned the science classroom down with my volcanic exhibition. Never did figure out why that teacher gave me a C just because he had to run to the window with a burning volcano and throw it outside. Looked pretty real to me. And it wasn't like the time I burned the kitchen cabinets because I forgot about the french-fry grease. I didn't get a grade on that endeavor, although my mom's response was very educational.

This was nothing like those incidents. I just burned a piece of paper on the playground. Then this brilliant idea leaped up from my twisted psyche. I called my friends over, assuring them that I had a really cool demonstration to show them. Looking at Duncan, one of the mean guys in the class, I said to him in my best "you're the lucky guy" tone, "Hold your hand out. I wanna show you something."

Duncan didn't leave his hand there very long. He chased me all around that playground! Some guys just can't take a joke.

GOOD AIM, GOD

What in the world does this have to do with intercession? Well, another translation of the word *paga* is "strike the mark." It's used this way in Job 36:32: "He covers His hands with the lightning, and commands it to *strike the mark*" (emphasis added). When God releases His light, causing it to flash forth from His presence like lightning, its striking the desired target is likened to intercession.

We're like a magnifying glass in one sense. No, we don't add to or magnify God's power, but we do let the "Son" shine through us, directing His light to desired situations, allowing it to "strike the mark."

Have you ever seen a tree struck by lightning? If so, you've seen a picture of intercession. I do lots of praying in woods nearby. At times I come across trees struck by lightning. The lightning is so hot that it literally changes the molecular structure of the trees and twists the trunks until they look like the stripes on a candy cane. The temperature in a lightning bolt can reach 30,000 degrees Celsius (45,000 degrees Fahrenheit)—hotter than the surface of the sun. That's hot stuff!

If I have my theology straight, the Creator must be greater than the creation. That means the power or energy in God is greater than a lightning bolt. No wonder the Scriptures say, "As wax melts before the fire, so let the wicked perish before God. . . . The mountains melted like wax at the presence of the Lord. . . . He raised His voice, the earth melted" (Pss. 68:2; 97:5; 46:6).

"For our God *is* a consuming fire" (Heb. 12:29, emphasis added).

IT'S IN THE BOOK

The Scriptures are full of imagery that associates God with light or lightning. Here are just a couple of instances (I've emphasized various words or phrases to call your attention to the theme of light):

And this is the message we have heard from Him and announce to you, that *God is light*, and in Him there is no darkness at all (1 John 1:5).

He is the sole expression of the glory of God [*the Light-being, the outraying or radiance of the divine*], and He is the perfect imprint and very image of [God's] nature, upholding and maintaining and guiding and propelling the universe by His mighty word of power. When He had by offering Himself accomplished our cleansing of sins and riddance of guilt, He sat down at the right hand of the divine Majesty on high (Heb. 1:3, *AMP*).

At times His light, or the release of it, is associated with His glory:

And an angel of the Lord suddenly stood before them, and *the glory of the Lord shone* around them; and they were terribly frightened (Luke 2:9).

And while He was praying, the appearance of His face became different, and *His clothing became white and gleaming. . . .* Now Peter and his companions had been overcome with sleep; but when they were fully awake, they saw His *glory* and the two men standing with Him (Luke 9:29,32, *NASB*; we read in the margin of the *NASB* that the word "gleaming" means literally, "*flashing like lightning*").

Sometimes this light, lightning, or glory of God is released from His mouth and often called a sword:

"Who alone possesses immortality and *dwells in unapproachable light*; whom no man has seen or can see. To Him be honor and eternal dominion! Amen."
—1 Timothy 6:16 (emphasis added)

Repent therefore; or else I am coming to you quickly, and I will make war against them with the *sword of My mouth* (Rev. 2:16).

And *from His mouth comes a sharp sword*, so that with it He may smite the nations; and He will rule them with a rod of iron; and He treads the wine press of the fierce wrath of God, the Almighty (Rev. 19:15).

The *voice of the Lord splits and flashes forth forked lightning* (Ps. 29:7, AMP).

If I whet My *lightning sword* and My hand takes hold on judgment, I will wreak vengeance on My foes and recompense those who hate Me (Deut. 32:41, *AMP*; think *Star Wars* was the first one to come up with the idea of a lightsaber? Think again!).

Other times, Scripture refers specifically to what God's light does in dealing with His enemies:

Fire goes before Him, and burns up His adversaries round about. *His lightnings lit up the world*; the earth saw and trembled (Ps. 97:3-4).

And there were *flashes of lightning* and sounds and peals of thunder; and there was a great earthquake, such as there

"And the city has no need of the sun or of the moon to shine upon it, *for the glory of God has illumined it, and its lamp is the Lamb*." —Revelation 21:23 (emphasis added)

had not been since man came to be upon the earth, so great an earthquake was it, and so mighty (Rev. 16:18).

And then there's the release of God's light in the context of saving His people:

And He sent out His arrows, and scattered them, and *lightning flashes* in abundance, and routed them (Ps. 18:14).

Flash forth lightning and scatter them; send out Thine arrows and confuse them (Ps. 144:6).

A BAD DREAM FOR YOU-KNOW-WHO

As you can gather from these and other fascinating Scriptures, God is light; and at times this light or glory flashes forth from Him as bolts of lightning. Many times the Bible says that to deal with His enemies—whether for Himself or for His people—God simply releases this glory or light into the situation. It flashes forth like lightning and *PAGA* HAPPENS! God's power "strikes the mark."

This happened once several thousand years ago when there was a coup attempt in heaven. Lucifer, inflated with pride, decided that he would exalt himself to God's position.

"Son of man, prophesy and say, 'Thus says the LORD.' Say, '*A sword, a sword* sharpened and also polished! Sharpened to make a slaughter, polished to *flash like lightning!*' . . . I have given *the glittering sword*. Ah! It is made for *striking like lightning*, it is wrapped up in readiness for slaughter." —Ezekiel 21:9-10,15 (emphasis added)

Bad idea.

This war lasted about as long as it takes for a lightning bolt to flash its brilliant light across the sky. Jesus said it this way in Luke 10:18-20 (my paraphrase): "Don't get excited, guys, just because demons are subject to you in My name. Big whoop. I watched Satan cast from heaven. It didn't take long—lightning flashed and he was gone. Get excited because you have a relationship with God."

We don't know that lightning literally flashed when Satan was ousted, but for some reason Jesus used this picture. He said it was "like lightning" (v. 18). The point isn't what can be seen with the human eye but what happens in the spiritual realm: Light overcomes darkness. And the light is more than a symbolic representation of God's goodness or purity; it represents His power or energy. So whether the lightning itself is literal or symbolic, the results are the same: God's power overcomes the kingdom of darkness.

I believe that Satan has some recurring nightmares, most of them involving lightning. One of them is probably a recurring, tormenting dream of when lightning flashed in heaven and he was kicked out. So you can imagine his horror when the light of God flashed forth at the Cross—the same light that had expelled him from heaven. Sorry, Satan, but that's a dream you'll be screaming from for the rest of eternity.

THE LIGHTNING ANOINTING

What does all this heavenly, lightning-filled activity have to do with our intercession? Everything. Because if intercession is pictured by God's lightning striking the mark; and if Christ's work of intercession when He met Satan, breaking his headship, was light overcoming darkness; and if our praying intercession simply releases or re-presents Christ's, then I think it's safe to say that our intercession releases the lightning of God to flash forth into situations, bringing devastation to the powers of darkness.

Remember the "bear anointing" and the "butterfly anointing" from a few chapters back? Maybe this is the "lightning anointing"! And the awesome thing is that the same light that overcame darkness is still blazing through us as the Holy Spirit shines.

In his first All-Star game, the legendary baseball pitcher Roger Clemens came to bat for the first time in years (he'd always played in the American League, which doesn't allow pitchers to hit). After watching a blazing fastball from Dwight Gooden whiz past him, Clemens turned and asked the catcher, Gary Carter, "Is that what my pitches look like?"

"You bet it is!" responded Carter.

From then on, Clemens pitched with far greater boldness, having been reminded of how a good fastball can be so overpowering to a hitter.[1]

We often forget how powerful the Holy Spirit in us is, how destructive to darkness is His lightning sword. It has supernatural power to overcome the works of darkness—when we release it with confidence.

MEETING GOLIATH ON BOURBON STREET

In an earlier chapter, I mentioned leading an outreach of 200 students from Christ for the Nations Institute to Mardi Gras. The majority of our ministry was on Bourbon Street, where most of the partying occurs. When it comes to darkness not only ruling but being overtly celebrated, it's hard to top that place.

We had prepared by spending many hours in prayer and preparation before going on this outreach and were assured in our hearts that we'd established victory in the Spirit. The light had preceded us. But claiming the spoils of this war wasn't without a few unforgettable battles, one of which involved a demonized man who intended to do some of us bodily harm—like *kill* us.

My partner and I had crossed Bourbon Street to speak with two of our students, who happened to be carrying a sign that read "God Loves You!" As we stood talking, a giant of a man, whom I'll call Goliath, came at us seemingly out of nowhere. He was about 10 feet tall (OK, about 6 feet 6 inches), weighed 500 pounds (OK, maybe 260). He was dressed from head to toe as a Roman soldier—or maybe as a Philistine soldier—and carried a long whip that he was cracking as he came up to us. His lips were covered with bloody froth and blood was trickling out of the corners of his mouth. Not a pretty sight, as evidenced by the crowd that quickly cleared the area. Goliath then began to shout in a deep, raspy voice, "God is love, huh? I'm gonna kill you!"

This is not good, I perceived quickly, being the genius that I am. As I stood wondering why one of the other three team members didn't do something, the reason suddenly occurred to me—I was the leader! So what was this courageous leader's response in the face of death? "Every man for himself!" I shouted, then ran as hard as I could.

OK, so that's not exactly how it went, but I'll have you know that I was scared out of my wits. What did I actually do? I *PAGA*'ed—big-time *paga*! And when I glanced at the other three, their lips were silently moving. They were *paga*'n too!

It was *paga* times four. Magnifying glass, don't fail me now!

As we stood and bound the powers of darkness in this man in the name of Jesus, within seconds he began to change. His countenance changed, his voice changed and his attitude changed. The demons controlling him had been overcome. Light prevailed. The man actually appeared confused. He looked at us with a strange expression, muttered something about going ahead with what we were doing and walked away slowly as the crowd watched in amazement.

Light overcame darkness. God's power "struck the mark" (*paga*), quieting the evil spirits and saving us from embarrassment and probable injury.

Later that night, as we all gathered and shared our war stories of the day, everyone was amazed as we related how fearless, confident and in control we were as Goliath confronted us. "Never a doubt," we assured the group. "Never a doubt." *Yeah, right!*

HOUSE OF GLORY

My father, Dean Sheets, who pastors in Ohio, saw light overcome darkness while on a missions trip to Haiti, where he was preaching the gospel and praying for the sick. The national religion of Haiti is voodoo, so demon activity is prominent and strong there. The powers of darkness have been given free rein.

On one occasion, Dad felt specifically led by the Holy Spirit to pray for blind individuals, so he invited them forward. Twenty people responded. As he stood before them one at a time, waiting for direction from the Holy Spirit, he was given the same instruction for 19 of the 20: "Cast out the spirit causing the blindness." Each time he did, the person was healed instantly, seeing perfectly.

Paga! Light striking the mark, penetrating darkened eyes, bringing sight.

What most believers don't realize is that these kinds of miraculous instances aren't just for bold evangelists or special missionaries. We are filled with the same glory and light that comes from God Himself. When the apostle Paul, inspired by the Holy Spirit, said, "Do you not know that you are a temple of God, and that the Spirit of God dwells in you?" (1 Cor. 3:16), he used the Greek word *naos* for "temple,"[2] which always referred to the holy of holies. He was literally saying, "Don't you know you are the holy of holies?"

The holy of holies was God's dwelling place back in the Old Testament temple days. Now we are that dwelling place—that house—where glory and light mingle, and God's power is free to shine forth.

As intercessors, it's crucial that we remember that the key to victory is carrying this presence of God into battle with us. He rises and scatters His enemies *through us*! We are soldiers of the light. We must boldly release the power of the Most High into situations, allowing the victory of Christ access. He has given us His light, He has given us His sword, He has given us His name. We can use them!

PRAYER IN PRACTICE

Holy God, You are victorious in battle. It's mind-boggling to think of the power that comes with just one word from You, let alone what You're made of. Lead me into battle, God, as I declare Your power, Your strength, Your might. May Your enemies be scattered as I pronounce Your goodness. Help me as I learn how to shine Your light into the dark areas of my life and those places in others' lives as well. Allow me to walk with the boldness of knowing that I am a soldier commissioned by You. Amen.

THINGS THAT MAKE YA GO HMM...

1. How are we like God's magnifying glass?
2. Explain how *paga* is related to lightning.
3. How is lightning a display of God's power to the forces of darkness?
4. Where and when can we shine God's light?
5. How can you transform a dark situation into one of light? Pray right now for God to give you specific strategy to transform a bad situation.

Notes

1. Craig Brian Larson, *Illustrations for Preaching and Teaching* (Grand Rapids, MI: Baker Books, 1993), p. 72, adapted.
2. Joseph Henry Thayer, *A Greek-English Lexicon of the New Testament* (Grand Rapids, MI: Baker Book House, 1977), p. 422.

THE SUBSTANCE
OF PRAYER

CHAPTER 12

TWO FROGS FELL INTO A CAN OF CREAM,
OR SO IT HAS BEEN TOLD.
THE SIDES OF THE CAN WERE SHINY AND STEEP,
THE CREAM WAS DEEP AND COLD.
"OH, WHAT'S THE USE," SAID NUMBER ONE,
"IT'S PLAIN NO HELP'S AROUND.
GOOD-BYE, MY FRIEND, GOOD-BYE, SAD WORLD"
AND WEEPING STILL HE DROWNED.

BUT NUMBER TWO, OF STERNER STUFF,
DOG PADDLED IN SURPRISE.
THE WHILE HE LICKED HIS CREAMY LIPS
AND BLINKED HIS CREAMY EYES.
"I'LL SWIM AT LEAST A WHILE," HE THOUGHT,
OR SO IT HAS BEEN SAID.
IT REALLY WOULDN'T HELP THE WORLD
IF ONE MORE FROG WERE DEAD.

AN HOUR OR MORE HE KICKED AND SWAM,
NOT ONCE HE STOPPED TO MUTTER.
THEN HOPPED OUT FROM THE ISLAND HE HAD
MADE OF FRESH CHURNED BUTTER.
(AUTHOR UNKNOWN)

Hang in there" didn't make it into the Ten Commandments, but it's one of the essential elements for an effective, praying Christian. In this day of instant everything—from fast foods to IMs to online term papers to T1 Internet connections—we are rapidly losing the character trait of hanging in there. We cook faster, travel faster, communicate faster, download faster, produce faster and spend faster—and we expect God to keep pace with us, especially in prayer.

We're like the African cheetah that must run down its prey to eat. It's well-suited for the task, as it can run at astonishing speeds of up to 70 miles per hour. But there's one problem: The cheetah has a disproportionately small heart, which causes it to tire after a short time. If it doesn't catch its prey quickly, it has to end the chase.

Many times we have the cheetah's approach in prayer. We zip into our prayer closets with tons of energy, we race to the front of the church with unbridled passion, or we speed to someone else for prayer. But lacking the heart for a sustained effort, we often stumble, and fail to follow through before we accomplish what's needed. So in our next prayer time, we decide to pray harder and faster, when what's needed may not be more explosive power but more staying power—stamina that comes only from a bigger prayer heart.

EASY DOESN'T DO IT

Even Jesus—God in flesh—spent many entire nights praying in order to fulfill His ministry. It took Him three arduous hours in Gethsemane to find strength to face the cross. We, on the other hand, have mastered the art of one-liners in prayer, and think

"It is not enough to begin to pray, nor to pray aright; nor is it enough to continue for a time to pray; but we must patiently, believingly, continue in prayer until we obtain an answer; and further we have not only to continue in prayer unto the end, but we have also to believe that God does hear us, and will answer our prayers. Most frequently we fail in not continuing in prayer until the blessing is obtained, and in not expecting the blessing." —George Müller

that if we give God a two-hour service once a week, then we're fairly spiritual. "Easy does it" might be good advice in a few situations, but for most of life, including prayer, easy *doesn't* do it.

A pilot early in a flight went to the back of the plane to check on the reason for a warning light. The problem was a door ajar, which flew open as he approached it. He was immediately sucked from the aircraft.

The copilot, seeing by his panel that a door was open, turned back toward the airport immediately and radioed for a helicopter to search the area. "I believe I have a pilot sucked from the plane," he said. After landing the plane, everyone was astonished to find the pilot holding on to the rung of a ladder, which he had miraculously managed to grab. He had held on for 15 minutes and, still more amazing, had managed to keep his head from hitting the runway, though it was only six inches away!

Upon finding the pilot, they had to pry his fingers from the ladder. That's perseverance![1]

Our American society has developed a severe problem. As we've become more immersed in a microwave culture where we get up-to-the-second information, we've lost the concept of waiting and persevering. And don't think it's not a problem among believers, many of whom give up if they haven't heard what they want from God in a matter of days. But like the frog, I've kicked and swum my way over time to more victories than I have accomplished quickly and easily. And I've found that a tenacious endurance is often the key to victory in prayer.

So What Are We Waiting For?

But *why*? Why is persistence or perseverance required in prayer? Does God have a certain amount of prayers required for certain situations? Do we talk Him into things? Does God ever "finally decide" to do something? Do we earn answers through hard work or perseverance?

Why did it take me 30 hours of praying to get the cyst dissolved on my wife's ovary? Why did it take a year to obtain a miracle for the little girl in the coma? Why does it sometimes demand several years of intercession to see someone saved? Why did Elijah have to pray seven times before the rain came? Why did Daniel have to pray 21 days before the angel broke through with his answer?

I'm sure there are a thousand different reasons why God places such value on praying persistently—999 of which I don't know. But I want to suggest one explanation for your consideration, something that Gordon Lindsay, a great man of prayer and the founder of Christ for the Nations, called the "substance" of prayer.[2]

So here it is: I believe that our prayers do more than simply motivate the Father to action; I believe that they actually release the power of the Holy Spirit from us to accomplish things. The fact that there's literal power from the Holy Spirit that can be released from us is just that—a fact. The power of God that brings life, healing and wholeness to the earth flows out from us as believers.

Many times we imagine God sitting on a throne in heaven and FedExing little packages of power down to Earth when we need it. The truth is, He's made His throne in our hearts. We are the temple of the Holy Spirit. As we discovered in the previous chapter, we are the holy of holies, the dwelling place of God on the earth. When He moves to release power upon the earth, it doesn't have to shoot out of the sky somewhere—it comes from His people, where His Spirit dwells upon the earth.

WHAT'S YOUR POWER MEASUREMENT?

It's also important to realize that this power is measurable. Certain amounts of this power must be released in the realm of the spirit to accomplish certain things. It's like the difference between the amount of power it takes to light a flashlight and the amount required to light a building, or a building as opposed to a city. The same thing is true in the spirit. Different amounts of God's power are needed to accomplish certain things.

MEASURES OF . . .

Did you know that there are measurable levels of almost any spiritual substance? There are measurable levels of faith. Romans 12:3 records the phrase, "as God has allotted to each a measure of faith." The word "measure" here is *metron*, from which we get the word "meter." In other words, God has "metered out" to each person a portion of faith; from there it must grow. There are measurable levels of faith, righteousness and grace. In Acts 4:33 (*NKJV*), we are told that "with great power the apostles gave witness to the resurrection of the Lord Jesus. And great grace was upon them all." The Greek word for "great" is *megas*, from which we get "mega." There's grace, there's mega grace and there's all grace (see 2 Cor. 9:8)!

There are measurable degrees of love. John 15:13 speaks of greater love. Matthew 24:12 talks of love that has grown cold. Philippians 1:9 refers to love abounding more and more. There are measurable degrees of the power of God. In Mark 6:5, there was a measurable degree of the power of God missing; because of the unbelief of the people in Nazareth, "He could do no miracle there." The Greek doesn't say, "He chose not to" or "He didn't." It literally says, "He could not" because their level of faith or unbelief had hindered the flow of the power of God. Although He was able to heal a few sick people, He couldn't work a miracle.

I'm convinced this is why it usually takes a while to get most prayers answered. Once in a blue moon, we'll receive an instant miracle. But typically it isn't just a matter of asking the Father to do something; rather it's a matter of releasing enough power in the spirit to get the job done. And sadly, most Christians aren't aware of this. After asking, we tend to sit back and wait on God, when, in fact, He's the one waiting on us. Our problem is that we've failed to understand that there are prayers that do more than just ask Him for things. Sometimes, when it appears that God has finally gotten around to it, or when we think something just suddenly happened, the truth is that enough power has finally been released through prayer to accomplish it.

PERSEVERING FOR THE POWER

Think about the prophet Elijah praying for rain in 1 Kings 18. We already talked about this story earlier in the book, but it's a perfect example of the importance of hanging in there when it comes to interceding for something. God told Elijah that He would send rain on the face of the earth. This wasn't the prophet's idea; it was *completely* God—His timing, His idea, His will.

If this was the case, then why in the world did Elijah have to pray seven different times until the rain came? If God initiated this whole thing, why didn't He just make it happen with a single word? The most reasonable explanation to me is that it was necessary for Elijah to persevere until he had completed enough prayer—until enough power had been released through his intercession to go up into the heavens and get the job done.

In the same way, why did it take Daniel 21 days to get his answer when God could have sent an angel to him the first day he started praying? Again, I believe that Daniel's faithful praying every day was releasing power into the realm of the spirit. Not until enough power was released to break through the demonic opposition in the spirit could God get His angelic messenger through with the answer!

Hear me out: I am in no way limiting God's power. I'm completely aware that one word from God could rout every demon in hell. But once again, it comes down to the fact that God has decided to work on Earth through humans. With that in mind, it seems reasonable to me that if a man's prayers were responsible for the angel being dispatched, they would also be the key to breaking through with the message.

PRAYING IN DELAY (DELAY, DELAY, DELAY)

I could go on and on explaining instances when I believe that God was waiting for prayers to be stored up in heaven in order to release enough power to do the job. Why did it take Jesus three hours in the Garden of Gethsemane to break through? Why didn't the angels come immediately and comfort Him? Because power was being released in the spirit to cause the breakthrough.

Why did it take a month to get rid of the cyst on my wife's ovary? Because power that was being released in the realm of the spirit was accomplishing something physically inside of her. Every day when that power was released, it was destroying the cyst just a little bit more . . . and more . . . and more.

Why did I have to pray for more than a year for the comatose girl I told you about at the beginning of this book? I went to see her at least once a week for a year, speaking the Word of God, weeping, calling forth a new brain inside of her head and fighting the good fight of faith. Why did it take a year? Because it takes a lot of power to form a new brain. Why didn't God do it instantly? I don't know. I tried everything I knew to get Him to do so.

I did all the things I'd read about the heroes of faith doing. In faith, I even sat her up in the bed and commanded her to wake up; but like a limp rag doll, she flopped back down on her pillow. I don't know why God chose not to do it as an instant miracle; but because He didn't, I'm relatively certain of this: A measurable amount of power had to flow until there was enough of it to produce that miracle.

TIPPING THE BOWLS OF HEAVEN

Clearly, the power source—God—isn't the problem here. Ephesians 3:20-21 gives us a clue as to what's holding up the process:

> Now to Him who is able to do exceeding abundantly beyond all that we ask or think, according to the power that works within us, to Him be the glory in the church and in Christ Jesus to all generations forever and forever. Amen.

Notice that verse 20 says that God is going to do way more than we could ever imagine "according to the power that works within us." That means that however much power we have stored up in us, that's the amount that can be released or distributed through our prayers. If we're low on power, then we can't expect our prayers to move mountains. It's foolish to think we'll see miracles when all we do is mutter a routine two-minute prayer every once in a while before school starts or flippantly toss up a few words to God throughout the day. We have to release the power of God inside of us on a consistent basis.

As we do this, the Scriptures indicate that our prayers accumulate. There are bowls in heaven in which our prayers are stored. Not one bowl for all of them, but "bowls." We don't know how many, but I think it's very likely that each of us has our own bowl in heaven. I don't know if it's literal or symbolic. It doesn't matter. The principle is still the same. God has something in which He stores our prayers for use at the proper time:

> And when He had taken the book, the four living crea-
> tures and the twenty-four elders fell down before the
> Lamb, having each one a harp, and golden bowls full of
> incense, which are the prayers of the saints (Rev. 5:8).

> And another angel came and stood at the altar, holding a
> golden censer; and much incense was given to him, that he
> might add it to the prayers of all the saints upon the gold-
> en altar which was before the throne. And the smoke of the
> incense, with the prayers of the saints, went up before God
> out of the angel's hand. And the angel took the censer; and
> he filled it with the fire of the altar and threw it to the
> earth; and there followed peals of thunder and sounds and
> flashes of lightning and an earthquake (Rev. 8:3-5).

According to these verses, either when He knows it's the right time to do something or when enough prayer has accumulated to get the job done, God releases power. He takes the bowl and mixes it with fire from the altar.

I want you to picture this: He takes the same fire that fell on Sinai, the same fire that burned the sacrifice consuming the rocks and water and everything else when Elijah was on the mountain, the same fire that fell at Pentecost, the same fire that destroys His enemies, the very fire of almighty God, and He mixes your bowl of prayers with His fire! Then He pours it upon the earth—lightning starts to flash, thunder crashes, the earth quakes. Something awesome happens in the realm of the spirit that then affects the natural realm.

How awesome is that?! It's most likely what happened when Paul and Silas were in jail and began to sing some late-night praises. Worship started ascending, God was anointing it, the bowls filled and God poured it out. The earth literally started quaking, the jail door opened and their shackles fell off. As a result, the first convert in Asia was born again in Philippi. The gospel made its first penetration into a new continent on Earth.

IT'S OUR JOB TO PRAY

Recently, I believe that the Lord showed me what sometimes happens when we come to Him with a need, asking Him to accomplish what He says in His Word. In answer to our requests, He sends His angels to get our bowls of prayer to mix with the fire of the altar. But often *there isn't enough in our bowls to meet the need!* Of course, our first response is usually to blame God or reason that it's not His will or that His Word must not really mean what it says. The reality is that sometimes He can't do what we've asked because we haven't given Him enough power in our prayer times to get it done. He's poured out all there was to pour and it wasn't enough! It's not just a faith issue, but it's also a power issue.

I hope this doesn't alarm you. I get excited when I think about it. I didn't know it at the time, but when I was standing over the comatose girl, every time I spoke the name of Jesus, every time I prayed in the Spirit, every time I laid hold of God's Word and promises, every tear I shed was put in a bottle (see Ps. 56:8)— or a bowl—and God was just watching until finally it was full.

And on a Saturday morning, the Almighty looked over at one of the angels and said, "See the little girl over there whose brain is no longer functioning and that has to be fed through her stomach and breathe through a hole in her throat and is lying there like a living dead person, and the doctors say there's no hope and that she's going to die? Do you see her? Take this bowl that's been filled, mix it with My fire, and go dump it on her head."

The rest is history—just as it will be for you as you fill bowls full of prayers for the miraculous!

PRAYER IN PRACTICE

Father, why is the thing I need the most the thing I do the least?
Why is it so easy to say I'm too busy to pray—really pray?
Lord, I humble myself before Your throne and ask You to
forgive me for my lack of prayer. Forgive me for the times I've
blamed You for not coming through with something I thought
should happen. Father, give me Your eyes to see more of how
this prayer thing really works in the spirit realm, not just in the
natural. I pray for the tenacity—the perseverance—that marks
a pray-er who catches Your ear every time I pray. Mold me into
a faithful intercessor for You and Your glory. Amen.

THINGS THAT MAKE YA GO HMM...

1. How do you think living in an ultrafast-paced society affects your prayer life and spiritual vision?
2. Why does God value perseverance in prayer so much?
3. Was the idea that spiritual things are measurable new to you? What other spiritual areas can you think of that can be measured?
4. Can you think of any situations when you may have stopped praying before your "bowl" was filled? Are there any current situations in your life that might need more power released to receive an answer?

Notes

1. Craig Brian Larson, *Illustrations for Preaching and Teaching* (Grand Rapids, MI: Baker Books, 1993), p. 114.
2. Gordon Lindsay, *Prayer That Moves Mountains* (Dallas, TX: Christ for the Nations, Inc., revised 1994), p. 43.

A VISION OF YOU

CHAPTER 13

A few years ago, I was in Washington, D.C., for the National Day of Prayer with the Master's Commission, a group of young people from Spokane, Washington. My wife, Ceci, and I went with them because, while I'd been ministering to them a couple of months prior, I had an incredible picture—I believe it was a vision. The picture was of a stadium filled with young people who were radically committed to God. As I watched, this multitude of young people filed out of the stadium and flooded the nation, taking revival with them.

I shared the picture with these young people, and a spirit of intercession came upon us that lasted for about 30 minutes. It was truly an awesome time of prayer for the youth of America. As we finished praying, I felt like I needed to join these young guys and gals on their upcoming trip to Washington, D.C.

Not long after we arrived in D.C., I sensed the Lord speak to me: *I'm going to confirm to you on this trip that I am sending revival to this nation. I'm also going to demonstrate to you that the youth will play a major role in it.*

WOULD YOU MIND CONFIRMING THAT?

My first confirmation came on The National Day of Prayer. There were probably 400 to 500 people gathered for the primary prayer meeting that morning—senators, congressmen, statesmen and spiritual leaders of the nation. I wasn't part of the program but was simply there to agree in prayer, as were most of the people attending. The Master's Commission had somehow received permission to be in the program, which was a miracle in itself. When these young people were invited up for their 15 minutes, they walked down the aisle singing "Heal Our Land."

As they sang, the Spirit of God fell over the room like a blanket. Perhaps "hovered" would be a better way to phrase it. At no other point was the presence of God felt as strongly. I didn't see anyone there who wasn't weeping. Dr. James Dobson, who spoke after The Master's Commission, commented through tears that we don't often get to witness history in the making. I'm sure that everyone in attendance believed that day impacted the history of our nation.

After the meeting, these young people met up with Norm Stone, a man from their church. God called Norm several years ago to walk across America seven times as a prophetic act of repentance and intercession for the babies murdered in America through abortion. *That's* prophetic action! The Master's Commission joined him for two weeks, walking behind him, and interceded for the unborn for 20 miles a day.

The night before these young people were to join Norm, I heard these words from the Lord: *This is a prophetic declaration by Me that the generation that Satan tried to annihilate through abortion—My next generation of warriors in the earth—have not and will not be destroyed. I'm sending these young people to march behind Norm as a prophetic message saying, "No! This is My generation, Satan, and you will not have them!"*

Later that evening, I heard the words: *I'm going to confirm to you once more that I'm sending revival to this nation, in which the youth will have a major role. I'll do it through the Bible reading you're to do tonight.*

I was scheduled to be part of a three-day read-a-thon—the entire Bible being read by individuals while facing the Capitol building. Each person participating was allowed to read for 15 minutes, no more. We were required to read from wherever the progression happened to be in the Bible when our turn came. I didn't pick my reading time—someone else had signed me up the previous day and informed me that I was supposed to be there at midnight the following night.

Due to the nature of the Lord's dealings with me at that time, I told Him, "Lord, there's only one way I could be certain that You're confirming these things to me through my Bible reading. When I arrive, have them tell me that I can either read the book of Habakkuk or Haggai." This wasn't a fleece, nor was I testing God. It was because of the things I had already sensed Him saying to me through these two books.

Do you know the size of these books? They consist of *eight pages* in my Bible. What would the odds be, when not choosing my own reading—nor even the time of my reading—of my showing up and someone telling me, "Here, read from these eight pages."

I walked up to the lady in charge.

"Are you Dutch Sheets?"

"Yes, I am."

"You're on in 15 minutes, after this person. You have your choice. You can either read the book of Haggai or the book of Habakkuk."

I nearly passed out! You can believe that I read the Word of the Lord with authority, making prophetic declaration over the government of this nation with absolute faith that revival is coming.

YES, WE HAVE HOMEWORK

Why am I telling you all this? Besides just simply being cool, it's a reminder to both you and me. I received those words—and the

"Every great movement of God can be traced to a kneeling figure." —D. L. Moody

confirmations—from God almost 10 years ago. Has revival come through the youth yet? Not really. There have been wonderful, amazing outbreaks in the past decade. God has moved radically among your age group, and I believe He's raising up the most outspoken, prophetic generation this Earth has ever seen. But unless I pulled a Rip Van Winkle and missed out, that massive revival—the "teens pouring out of stadiums" kind of revival—hasn't hit yet.

When I think of what that means, it stirs me in the deepest places, and I hope it does the same for you. From what we've learned in this book, I think it's safe to say that the bowls aren't filled yet. God is still waiting for more of us to take this seriously, to pray with fervancy, precision and perseverance. He's longing for the day when He can tip those heavenly containers and douse us all with an overwhelming outpouring of His Holy Spirit. But until that day, here's our assignment: pray, pray, pray!

God is calling the Church—and especially the teen generation—to a new understanding of prophetic action and declaration, functioning as His voice and Body upon the earth. When He speaks His plan to us, however foolish it may seem—to hold up a rod, speak to the spiritually dead, walk our neighborhoods, march through our streets, hit rocks, decree to the earth, lay hands on and speak to oppressive walls, walk across America, read the Bible toward the Capitol, speak to a nation that isn't listening—He needs us to DO IT!

The Lord may lead you to anoint the hallways of your school with oil, pray over classrooms, or do some other symbolic act that seems crazy at the time. But whatever He says to you, do it. Be bold to declare His Word over and into situations. Don't be scared of the opposition that awaits you—expect it! Our task would be overwhelming if it weren't for the fact that this is all about God in the first place. We're not relying on our own strength; we're counting on God's. With God on their side, Gideon's 300 were more than enough to defeat 135,000. So if He's for us, seriously, who can successfully be against us (see Rom. 8:31)?

Let's do it! Let's let God arise and His enemies be scattered. Let's fill our bag with the stones of victory and run to meet Goliath. Let's demonstrate the awesomeness of our God. Let's growl! Let's roar! Let's let Jesus live through us.

He's ready—are you?

Are you ready to walk in your calling as an intercessor? To represent Jesus as the reconciler and the warrior? To distribute His benefits and victory? To meet, to carry away, to set boundaries?

Are you ready to birth, to liberate, to strike the mark? To fill some bowls, to make some declarations, to watch and pray?

Are you ready?

Remember: Life is fragile, handle with *PAGA!*

PRAYER

Lord God, help me to be worthy of Your calling on my life to represent You and pray Your will on Earth. By Your Holy Spirit, enable me to persevere in the heavenlies. Thank You that You've called me to intercede for Kingdom matters rather than for just meaningless stuff. You are awesome, and I worship You. Send me out now with Your anointing. Amen.

THINGS THAT MAKE YA GO HMM . . .

1. What has God called you to do when it comes to prayer and intercession?
2. Who are three people that can join you in interceding for your school? (Set up a regular time to meet with them and pray.)
3. How can God use your generation to change this nation for the better?

DISCUSSION

LEADER'S GUIDE

One of the greatest aspects of learning about intercessory prayer is being able to join with other believers on the journey. No one person hears, discerns or knows *all* of what God wants to do at a certain time; that's the beauty of how He created His Body, with its various and essential parts each having distinct functions. In other words, you may be sensing the Holy Spirit saying one thing during a time of intercession, while someone else may be hearing something completely different. Yet both have value in the Kingdom and in our response to God's prompting.

And that's where you, the group leader, come in. As a leader, it's important to be sensitive to the maturity level of the group. It's also important that you don't impose your beliefs on those who differ in the way they worship the Lord. Establish an environment of openness and discovery. Allow people to share their opinions, experiences, insights, etc. And set a common goal: *To grow in your walk with the Lord as it pertains to prayer.*

Group discussion is exactly that—it's a *group* thing. Be careful to not dominate conversation, yet be just as alert for others who may have the tendency to do the same. Go out of your way to include those who are reluctant to speak up, and make it a fun time for everyone involved.

ON THE PRACTICAL SIDE

Ideally, your group will have about 10 to 15 people. A smaller group can make for struggles along the way when people aren't able to attend; a larger group often requires strong leadership skills on your part to create a sense of belonging and meaningful participation for each person. Whatever the size of your group, the important thing is that you're all on the same page, which is what you, the leader, can facilitate.

If you're planning to study this book as an extended series for a Sunday School class or small group, first decide how many weeks to set aside. Make sure that you allow enough time during each session to both cover the material and share personal discoveries. And it never hurts to bring in relevant examples from daily life. Keep your eyes open to any daily events, cultural trends or current movies, TV shows, songs, etc., that can be applied to what you're learning.

As you begin the series, it's crucial in the first session to create a sense of unity and involvement for each person. The subject matter of Chapter 1 is light enough to not turn people away, yet it should also invoke plenty of discussion. To prompt some reaction, consider asking one or more of the following questions:

1. On a scale of 1 to 10, how would you rate your prayer life? How do you think God would rate it?
2. What are some of your strengths when it comes to prayer? What are some areas in which you think you could improve?
3. What do you hope to gain from studying this book?
4. If you could ask God one question about prayer, what would it be?

Throughout the weeks, you may want to allow a time during meetings in which group members can anonymously write out any questions or issues that haven't been tackled so far. As you conclude the series, you can compile these questions and have a generic "Q & A" time in which you address any questions that weren't answered during your meeting times.

Here are some other pointers to consider as you lead your group:

1. **Don't play the teacher.** Arrange seating to create a casual atmosphere. Avoid a setting that has you standing "in front" of the group leading—this usually squelches group participation.

2. **And don't play the savior.** The purpose of this study is to learn how to pray more effectively. It's not about fixing personal problems, as much as you might want to help do that with some members of your group. While you can be honest and sincere with your advice, try not to come across as a know-it-all with every solution. Instead, challenge participants throughout the study to use each lesson as impetus to pray for healing, strength, protection, etc.

3. **Listen first.** Receive statements from group members without judgmentalism, even if you disagree with them. Obviously, when dealing with teens, there are times where you'll need to keep people on track or simply state the truth to avoid time being wasted. But rejecting a comment outright will only stifle the group. Instead, try to clarify the issue by stating biblical truth.

4. **Be willing to deviate—a little.** If someone asks a question or comments on something off subject, either suggest that it be dealt with at another time or ask the group if they want to pursue the new issue now.

5. **Control the dominator.** If one person monopolizes the discussion, direct a few questions specifically to someone else. Again, be careful not to squelch any eagerness to voice thoughts or opinions; but also make sure that everyone has a fair chance to express themselves.

6. **You don't know everything . . . so admit it.** Teens will appreciate your authenticity when you acknowledge the fact that you don't have all the answers. Obviously, you don't have to go to the other extreme in playing dumb. But when you come across a tough question that you're unable to answer, tell the group that you'll get back with them the following week, and then follow through with your promise.

7. **Pray.** It's a no-brainer, but you'd be amazed how often people study *about* prayer yet somehow "forget" to actually do it when they meet as a group. Make sure to allot time each session to pray specifically through what's been discussed in that week's lesson. Then allow teens to offer up their prayer requests, and have them pray for each other.

8. **Do it daily.** Each week, assign individuals another group member to pray for each day of that week. This will perpetuate a sense of unity and love.

9. **Cover your group.** As a leader, pray regularly for the sessions and for the participants, asking the Holy Spirit to hover over each person throughout the week. The Lord will honor your willingness to guide His people toward a more intimate relationship with Him.

OTHER BOOKS BY
DUTCH SHEETS

Intercessory Prayer
How God Can Use Your Prayers to Move Heaven and Earth

Watchman Prayer
How to Stand Guard and Protect Your Family, Home and Community

How to Pray for Lost Loved Ones

The River of God
Moving in the Flow of God's Plan for Revival

Tell Your Heart to Beat Again
Let the Whispers of God Bring New Hope to Your Soul

God's Timing for Your Life
Seeing the Seasons of Your Life Through God's Eyes